FAMILIES IN WEYBOURNE FROM THE 17TH TO THE 20TH CENTURIES

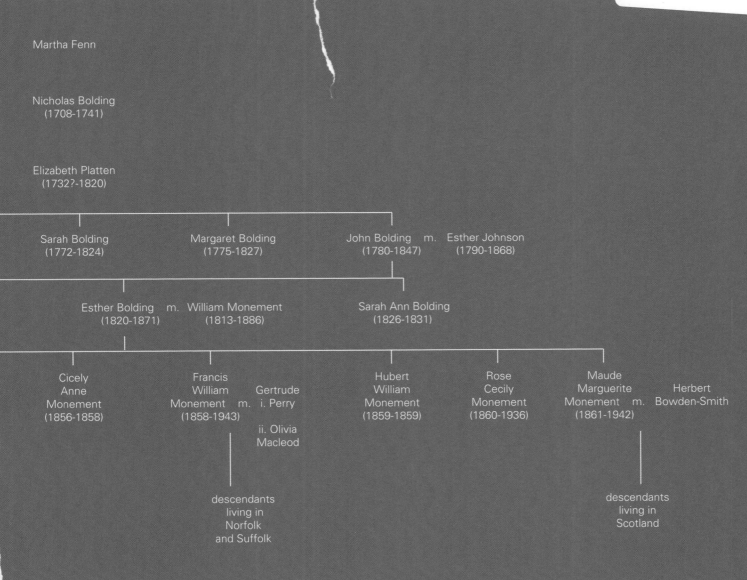

Martha Fenn

Nicholas Bolding
(1708-1741)

Elizabeth Platten
(1732?-1820)

Sarah Bolding
(1772-1824)

Margaret Bolding
(1775-1827)

John Bolding   m.   Esther Johnson
(1780-1847)   (1790-1868)

Esther Bolding   m.   William Monement
(1820-1871)   (1813-1886)

Sarah Ann Bolding
(1826-1831)

Cicely
Anne
Monement
(1856-1858)

Francis
William
Monement   m.
(1858-1943)

Gertrude
i. Perry

ii. Olivia
Macleod

Hubert
William
Monement
(1859-1859)

Rose
Cecily
Monement
(1860-1936)

Maude
Marguerite
Monement   m.
(1861-1942)

Herbert
Bowden-Smith

descendants
living in
Norfolk
and Suffolk

descendants
living in
Scotland

A Victorian Gentleman's
North Norfolk

The Watery Landscape

A Victorian Gentleman's
North Norfolk

WJJ Bolding and his place in early photography

Richard Jefferson

To Pauline
W.J.J. Bolding's great great niece

All proceeds from the sale of this book are going in support of Big C
Norfolk & Waveney's own cancer charity, in memory of Pauline

Copies of this book can be purchased from the Big C office:

10a Castle Meadow
Norwich NR1 3DE
Tel: 01603 619990

Big C have opened a centre at King's Lynn at 32 Norfolk Street PE30 1AH
and copies of the book will be available from there.

Copies can be purchased from Richard Jefferson
Oak Lodge
4 Woodlands Close
Holt
Norfolk NR25 6DU

richardjefferson@f2s.com

Copies can also be purchased from the publisher.

ISBN 978-1-899163-78-6
Copyright © 2013 Richard Jefferson
First published 2013

Published by
JJG Publishing
Sparrow Hall
Hindringham
Norfolk NR21 0DP
Designed by Graham Hiles
Printed in China through Colorcraft Ltd, Hong Kong

Contents

Acknowledgements

Without access to all the best of WJJB's photographs there would, of course, be no book. My late wife Pauline's collection contained only a limited number of fine examples. It is the kindness of other family members in allowing me to use their photographs that requires me to express my thanks most sincerely: to Elizabeth Leslie (a great great niece of WJJB), who has the most extensive collection of all in the north of Scotland; to my brother-in-law Paul Long (a great great nephew of WJJB), whose album of early examples is very special; to Malcolm Bolding Paton (a great great nephew of WJJB), living in Weybourne and his son Nigel (great great great nephew) living in the U.S.A. for their oil paintings and photographs; to Mary Athill for her photographs of the Hamond and Charles Darwin connection. Picture Norfolk, in the Norfolk and Norwich Millennium Library, hold a small quantity of original photographs, as well as a considerable number of high quality sepia prints made by the late Cliff Middleton many years ago. The images on pages 28, 53, 74, 87, 108, 113 and 141 are courtesy of Norfolk County Council Library and Information Service.

John Benjafield, who is an expert on early photography, has been the most enormous help to me over the last ten years or so while I have been trying to piece together details of WJJB's life. My efforts have been patchy, to say the least. On occasions six months have gone by (normally in the summer, with long days, warm weather and the cricket season) and no progress has been made. John has encouraged me throughout, cajoled me, and nursed me, and I'm extremely grateful for everything he has done. His belief, all along, that WJJB and his photography is fully worthy of a book, has spurred me on. I knew from the start that my critical judgement is flawed, so John's chapter on WJJB as a photographer, within the context of the first days of photography, is of huge importance for any success the book may have*. Thank you John very much indeed.

---

* The captions for the 'First Eleven' photographs, and most of the 'Second Eleven' are also his.

Not only did I have to have access to the best photographs, it was essential to have them photographed expertly. It is extremely useful having a son who is a professional photographer, so thank you Rupert for all your efforts in digitalising over four hundred items for consideration for inclusion in the book: photographs, art work, archaeology etc. Included was a two-day trip up to Inverness from Gatwick with Easy Jet. You should be very proud of the result.

As someone who has never been anywhere near book production before, I have felt, at times, like someone wandering round with a blindfold on. My good fortune has been to use Jeremy (Quill) Greenwood (a good friend for over forty years) as publisher for the book. He has over fifty years experience in book publishing (over thirty years as Quiller Press and, latterly, as JJG Publishing) who has led me forward at each stage. The layout of the book has been in the hands of Graham Hiles. He has been patient with me in the extreme all the way through. My sincere thanks to both you gentlemen for enabling my ambition to be fulfilled.

Chapter 1

Introduction

For more than sixty years of the 19th century Queen Victoria ruled as queen of the British people, and, as the century progressed, as queen of the new colonies, the British Empire. Such was the length of her reign and such was the 'greatness' of her nation and empire, that historians talk of 'Victorian Britain' and the 'Victorian Age'.

A HISTORY LESSON

I have in my possession a box, which has come down through the family, containing small watercolour representations, drawn on thick card, of all the English monarchs (and Oliver Cromwell) from William the Conqueror in 1066 up to Queen Victoria's reign. Nine events from each reign could be placed over the blank circles on each. The young Queen Victoria has 'Crimean War' (1854-1856), 'Duke of Wellington died' (1852), 'Sepoy War' (1857) among the events of the early part of her reign that are recorded. It was WJJB who created these fascinating aids to History education for his nine nephews and nieces, the children of his sister Esther.

Queen Victoria lived from 1819 to 1901. The subject of this book William Johnson Jennis Bolding (hereafter referred to as WJJB) had an almost identical lifespan to that of his monarch. He lived from 1815 to 1899, so he was a Victorian through and through. His active adult years were the years of great progress with the Industrial Revolution and many life-changing inventions, but his own life was lived far from the hustle and bustle of the new age. He died in the house in which he was born, in a small coastal village in north Norfolk, almost all his life's work and achievements taking place within a few miles of his home. Such, and varied, were his talents, that he can surely be described as a truly remarkable man.

> **WEYBOURNE** – The death occurred on Saturday (October 21st 1899), in his eighty-fourth year, of Mr William Johnson Jennis Bolding, a well-known inhabitant of the parish. The deceased, who had been in failing health for some years, will be much missed, especially by his poorer neighbours, amongst whom his kindly nature and unostentatious charity had won for him universal respect and esteem. He added to considerable scientific attainments artistic powers of no mean degree, and besides having travelled a great deal in early life, he was widely read in the literature of the day, especially as concerned archaeological subjects.
>
> (*The Norfolk Chronicle and Norfolk Gazette* 28th October 1899)

This newspaper notice is the only evidence we have regarding the character of WJJB. No letters survive, no diary, no writing of his except an archaeological report and a few isolated archaeological notes. Surely he must have written extensively; so many of the educated middle-class Victorians did. Legend in his village of Weybourne in north Norfolk has it that on an occasion in the first half of the 20th century, most likely after a descendent of WJJB died, there was a bonfire in the garden of effects from the house that burnt for a week. What treasures of evidence were destroyed is anyone's guess. The lack of evidence has made it impossible for me to write a conventional biography of WJJB. He was an outstanding early photographer, being introduced to the art within ten years of its invention, and this book is being written because of his photography, and his place in the history of photography. His portrait photographs of his family and the village people of Weybourne deserve to be seen by a wide audience; he deserves wide recognition. He was also a talented amateur artist with connections with members of the Norwich School, and he had a wide range of other leisure interests. On top of that he had extensive business interests in his home village of Weybourne and the surrounding north Norfolk area.

Jennis Bowden-Smith, an unmarried great-niece of WJJB, and my late wife Pauline's first cousin once removed, lived in 'The Cottage', Weybourne, almost opposite WJJB's home, 'The House' (now the Maltings hotel). WJJB in his will left 'The Cottage' to his four unmarried nieces (see the Bolding/Monement family tree endpapers). Jennis Bowden-Smith inherited 'The Cottage' on the death of the last of the four sisters, her aunts, in 1936. 'The Cottage' was a misleading name, because the property consisted of eleven bedrooms. Built in the 17th century, as a small cottage, it had been added to, again and again, in the second half of the 19th century until reaching its present proportions by 1899 when WJJB died. His youngest sister Esther had married a King's Lynn merchant William Monement and had given birth to eleven children in fifteen years between 1846 and 1861.

After her death in 1871 her family spent more and more time in Weybourne. After their father's death in 1886, their uncle's village became their permanent home. It is reported that WJJB's four nieces lived in separate wings of the house, but had a communal room in which they came together when they felt so inclined. This is what Jennis inherited, along with furniture, pictures and personal effects that had once belonged to WJJB, and she lived there on her own for the rest of her life – more than forty years.

To what extent Jennis knew of the importance of the treasures in her house is not

'The Cottage' before any additions. c1860.

'The Cottage'. c1995.

recorded, but by 1970 she was in failing health, crippled with rheumatoid arthritis and with very poor eyesight. I remember Pauline and I visiting cousin Jennis from the middle of the 1960s onwards, but despite her disabilities, she retained a lively interest in people and everything around her. A near neighbour of hers, Brigadier J.F.M.(Derick) Mellor, a recently-retired distinguished career soldier, visited her regularly and helped her with her correspondence and with paying her bills for her. On one visit he was asked to find something in a cupboard. It was then that he came upon a sackful of old letters at floor level, a number of which were ruined by damp; also Victorian scrapbooks on the shelves, sketchbooks, a journal and old photographs. On subsequent visits more and more, and yet more, items came to light as Jennis guided him into long forgotten nooks and crannies.

Derick Mellor was fascinated with local history and by the time his first fifteen years of retirement were over and failing health had set in, he had researched a huge range of subjects around north Norfolk and had written, along with other publications, over a hundred articles for a monthly local parish magazine. WJJB, his family and linked events, were woven into a number of the articles. This was in the future, but in Weybourne in the early 1970s he struck on the idea of writing some articles on Jennis's ancestors, with WJJB just referred to as 'great-uncle William', using the material he had unearthed. In order to keep Jennis involved, and to give her an interest to cheer her life up, they would be written as if by her and signed 'Jennis'.

With this in mind he contacted the editor of *Norfolk Fair* (the county and regional magazine with 80,000 readers) and invited him out to lunch. Not surprisingly the editor was won over, particularly by the superb photographs of local characters. These he borrowed to take to show to Cliff Middleton, a professional photographer and expert on early Norfolk photography. They were identified as 'Albumen prints taken from calotype negatives – date c1855'. The editor and Cliff Middleton, in a state of high excitement, then went up to Weybourne to copy a large number of photographs from which to choose for the articles.

Three articles appeared in *Norfolk Fair*; the first (January 1974) mainly used family letters dating from the 1780s and 1790s. The second (November 1974) and third (December 1974) threaded together many stories told by Jennis's grandmother Esther in her journal in the years before her marriage. Sadly the journal has disappeared; it would have been a very valuable source for evidence about WJJB's early life. Parts of Derick Mellor's articles, including his extracts from the journal, will be borrowed later.

At the same time as Derick Mellor was working on his articles, Cliff Middleton was taking WJJB's portrait photographs to London to show them to experts at the National Portrait Gallery and elsewhere. This resulted in two of his photographs, 'William Cooke, jobbing gardener' and 'Woman, Weybourne Village, Norfolk' being included in the 1975 Arts Council of Great Britain travelling exhibition 'The Real Thing – An Anthology of British Photographs 1840-1950.' W.H. Fox Talbot, Hill and Adamson, Roger Fenton, Henry Peach Robinson, Julia Margaret Cameron are all there in the catalogue and, as to WJJB, it was stated that his 'photographs of his estate workers and the village people of Weybourne are amongst the most powerful portraits in the history of photography'.

Jennis Bowden-Smith died in May 1977, but not before sanctioning an exhibition of WJJB's photographs and memorabilia which was held from 15th July to 3rd September in the Museum of Social History, 27 King Street, King's Lynn. At the launch Cliff Middleton gave a talk: 'W.J.J.Bolding – A Country Photographer'. The September 1977 issue of *Norfolk Fair* printed a transcript of his talk. In the October 1977 issue 'The Country Portraits of William Bolding' showed photographs of

Illustrated in the catalogue of 'The Real Thing' 1975 page 11 – 'Woman, Weybourne Village, Norfolk'. It is thought that she might be Billy Cooke's wife. c1855.

'**William Cooke, jobbing gardener**'. William (Billy) Cook (Cooke), WJJB's gardener. This photograph was exhibited in 1856, 1975 and 2003.

village people, with Middleton writing that 'these are almost certainly the first photographs of Norfolk people ever taken and certainly one of the earliest (comprehensive) photographic records of rural dress and trades taken anywhere in the world.' The *Norfolk Fair* editor in his September editorial commented that 'he (WJJB) has blossomed by their efforts (Derick Mellor and Cliff Middleton) from total obscurity to national importance.'

A huge debt is owed to Derick Mellor for all his efforts in bringing WJJB from total obscurity into the public domain. Without him, who knows, when Jennis died in 1977, WJJB's photographs may well have just been transferred within the family with no recognition of their importance, or they might have been removed in a house clearance, ended up in a skip, or been burnt. Derick kept me in touch with all that he was doing on a regular basis, but with my work as a school master and with a young family I was not able to show more than a passing interest at that time. Cliff Middleton's expertise also played an important part in promoting WJJB.

Time moved on again. WJJB the photographer disappeared from view once more. In 1997 Derick Mellor died aged 84. Cliff Middleton had retired

Left. Unknown man. c1855.

Right. Joe Digby, wearing a moleskin waistcoat over a slop and shirt. c1855.

1 Charles English, seen holding leather hedging gloves or Darnocks and a hedging bill. c1855.

2 Piper Digby. c1855.

3 Guffy Digby, farm labourer. c1855.

4 Bob Lyne. c1855.

to Tuscany, where he died in November 2000, by which time there were three WJJB photographs in the Eaton Collection in the Norwich Library photo-archive, purchased by the Norfolk County Council. These three photographs were on display in an important exhibition 'A Period Eye' held in Norwich Castle from September 2003 to February 2004, with 'William Cooke, Jobbing Gardener' on the cover of the catalogue (*see photograph on page 6*). This was the same photograph that had been shown in Norwich in 1856, and in the Arts Council of Great Britain 1975 travelling exhibition. The other two photographs were 'Photographic Studio, Weybourne' (*see photograph page 76*) and 'Portrait of an unknown man' (*see photograph page 87*). John Benjafield in the catalogue wrote of the latter that 'this photograph shows Bolding's mastery of the techniques of the close-up. The anonymous subject possesses one of the most distinctive necks in the whole of photography.'

Chapter 2

A Gentleman Amateur – W.J.J. Bolding and Early Photography in Norfolk

by John Benjafield

Photography emerged in the western world long after its key elements became known. The optical principle of the *camera obscura* was known in the 4th century BC and portable versions were available in the 17th century. In 1725, Johann Schulze discovered silver salts were sensitive to sunlight so, we may ask, why did it take another hundred years before photography really started to emerge?

Before photography, the natural world was interpreted and represented by artists and draughtsmen sometimes using perspectival machines such as the pantograph, the physionotrace and the *camera obscura*. Printed and pictorial media such as painting, engraving, etching and lithography fed a growing appetite to make sense of our world and enrich our experience of it. Many artists strived for 'realism' but it was exacting, time-consuming and costly. The growth of scientific knowledge was, in some ways, inhibited by the lack of accurate copies of natural specimens and in the early 19th century there was a growing realisation of the need for rapid, 'real' pictorial representation. Henry Talbot wrote of his motivation to discover a way for 'natural images to imprint themselves durably, and remain fixed upon the paper!' Nicéphore Niépce, in France, also wrote a memoir on his 'long researches on the method of fixing the image of objects by the action of light alone.' There were many others in the west who were working to this end but photography was not finally publicly announced until 1839 by Louis Daguerre in France and Henry Talbot in England. The Daguerreotype and the Photogenic Drawing were made by very different processes but they opened a new era in our visual cultural evolution.

Louis Daguerre, a fine-art painter, showman and inventor of the Diorama, attracted huge audiences to his Diorama where he presented vast transparent paintings illuminated with changing lighting effects, so it's not surprising that he was drawn to considering how fugitive images might be made permanent. He became serious about this in 1829 when he cleverly negotiated a partnership with Nicéphore Niépce who had invented heliography (c. 1822). This was a very slow process where an image projected in a *camera obscura* caused relative hardening of a thin layer of bitumen of Judea on glass. The unhardened bitumen was washed away with oil of lavender and white petroleum and the remaining hardened bitumen formed the picture which could not be changed by further exposure to light. Niépce and Daguerre experimented separately in attempts to improve the process as Daguerre later wrote '… as regards rapidity, sharpness of the image, delicate gradation of the tones, and above all the perfection of the details…' In 1833 Niépce died suddenly, leaving Daguerre to continue his experiments to achieve their stated objective. By 1837

Louis Daguerre.
E. Thiesson, Daguerreotype, 1844.

Daguerre's experiments resulted in a very different process of making and fixing the image. In January 1839 he made his sensational public announcement about his Daguerreotype. He had succeeded in making a unique, positive image in a silver amalgam on a copper plate. A carefully polished, silvered copper plate was sensitised to light by exposure to fumes of iodine and bromine. The sensitised plate was then exposed in a camera and the latent image formed was developed by exposure to fumes of hot mercury and fixed with 'hypo' (sodium hypo-sulphate). The image formed was a unique, monochrome, direct positive of very high resolution. It was also very fragile and was

'L'Atelier de l'artiste'.
Louis Daguerre, Daguerreotype, 1837.

Henry Talbot.
Antoine Claudet, Daguerreotype, c 1845.

usually protected with a glass cover in a case or framed. Early viewers sometimes called them 'magic mirrors'. Daguerre delayed publishing the details of his process until August of that year and secured a patent for it in England, Wales and the British Colonies.

When Henry Talbot, resident at Lacock Abbey, near Bath in Wiltshire, heard the news of Daguerre's invention, he was galvanised into action and immediately set about staking his claim to have independently invented the process of photography.

Talbot, a Cambridge graduate, was elected Fellow of the Royal Society in 1831 and served briefly as a Member of Parliament. The upbringing and talents of Daguerre and Talbot were strikingly different. Whereas Daguerre was an artist and impresario, Talbot's interests ranged across Assyriology, astronomy, botany, etymology, mathematics and optics. He was motivated to 'fix' fugitive images as he felt disillusioned at not being a competent artist when using an optical aid called a *camera lucida*. In 1834 he began experimenting by sensitising paper to light using silver salts and obtained 'photogenic drawings' of such things as grass [*see above*] by contact printing them using sunlight. By 1835 he captured his

Left: Ricardi Secundi.
Henry Talbot, photogenic drawing, 1839.
Right: Agrostis Gigantea
Henry Talbot, photogenic drawing, 1839.

first 'in camera' image of an Oriel window at Lacock Abbey.

He made his photogenic drawings first by floating paper on a solution of sodium chloride (common salt) and when the paper dried he brushed it with silver nitrate solution. The two chemicals reacted to form silver chloride and only those areas of the paper exposed to light went dark. This is called a 'printing-out' process. He found that he could stabilise the dark image in the paper by washing it with a strong salt solution. What he had made was a negative image, one with reversed tonality. Immediately he knew that he could print a positive image from it by allowing sunlight to pass through the paper negative in contact with another sensitised paper In order to back up his claim to have invented photography, Talbot arranged an exhibition of his photogenic drawings on 25th January 1839 and revealed the details of his process to The Royal Society. Talbot's exhibits predated Daguerre's images by some two years but, of course, they approached their subject in very different ways and the activities of both men were unknown to each other.

Talbot soon improved his technique with the invention of the Calotype negative in which a latent image formed, after a short exposure time in camera, and was 'developed out' in a solution of gallic acid, silver nitrate and acetic acid. He then increased the translucence of the negative using paraffin wax and printed positives from it. These positives were 'fixed' using sodium hyposulphite ('hypo', now known chemically as sodium thiosulphate). The positive prints made from these negatives were called *salted paper prints*. Needless to say, Talbot patented his Calotype process which, it can be argued, slowed down the growth of photography.

Although the fragile Daguerreotype image offered very high definition, it was the continuous improvement of Talbot's lower definition, negative/positive process which ultimately displaced the Daguerreotype and was used for making photographs until the last quarter of the 20th century.

Whereas many painters were greatly alarmed by what they thought was '*a bastard left by science on the doorstep of art*', many others in the fields of science and trade found immediate benefits.

Frederick Scott Archer.
by Robert Cade, c 1855.

Wet glass-plate collodion process

In 1851, the Englishman Frederick Scott Archer introduced a practical process for making photographic negatives on glass. A sensitised glass plate in a wooden frame (called the dark slide) was fitted into the back of a camera and was then exposed to the subject to be photographed, removed from the camera and chemically developed while still wet. Although cumbersome, it produced very high resolution negatives and was known as the wet collodion process. In fact, making collodion is not without risks as it is made by dissolving gun-cotton (cellulose nitrate) in a mixture of alcohol and ether. Gun-cotton has caused the deaths of many who handled it without due care. The collodion was sensitised with silver nitrate in a small bath and, after in-camera exposure to the subject, was developed using ferrous sulphate. Liquid collodion, invented in 1846, had been used for dressing and protecting wounds as it dried to form a clear thin film and was later used in the Crimean War.

The albumen print

In 1850, Louis Désiré Blanquart-Evrard advanced photographic printing by inventing a process of suspending the sensitising solution in a thin layer of egg white on the paper base. This is known as the albumen print and, as the silver salts did not flow into the fibres of the paper, the image produced by contact printing was much sharper than that from a paper negative.

Early Norfolk photography

As early as 1840, Daguerreotypes were on show at the Norwich Polytechnic Exhibition. Mrs. Opie (Amelia Opie, writer and anti-slavery activist) showed one and the London Polytechnic Institution exhibited five. Mrs Barwell, in her 'Companion' to the exhibition, says that examples of Photogenic Drawings were also on display but were not listed in the catalogue.

It's notable that Henry Harmer, a Great Yarmouth solicitor, contributed four photographs to the 1851 Great Exhibition held in London but it was not until the 1852 Norwich Polytechnic Exhibition that Daguerreotypes

Sparrow's House [Ipswich].
by Robert Cade, c 1855.

and photographs were again exhibited in Norfolk. Susannah Smith, resident in Lakenham, advertised her business both as artist and photographer offering 'Daguerreotype or Sun Pictures' and chose to show Daguerreotypes. James Howes, a printer and bookbinder at Back of the Inns, exhibited photographs which were printed from collodion, glass plate negatives.

The Great Exhibition had stimulated interest in promoting photography as a discrete subject and the Photographic Society of London was founded in 1853. In June 1854 the Norwich Photographic Society was founded and within 12 months it had 50 members. In 1856 it held a major exhibition to display their talents and those of photographers from other regions, including overseas. WJJB entered four architectural prints in this show and a Norfolk News review read '*Mr WJJ Bolding's pictures are perhaps the finest proofs we have seen from waxed paper on account of the unusual transparency of the pictures.*'

Self portrait.
Blanquart-Evrard, 1869.

To see WJJB's photographs in historical perspective it's necessary briefly to explore the work of other photographers in the Norfolk area. The earliest significant collections are in the archives of the Heritage Centre, Norfolk and Norwich Millennium Library and the Norfolk Record Office. Photographs printed from paper negatives dating from 1845 by Thomas Eaton show his talents in portraiture and cityscapes. These small, painterly, often faded images record details of his world in a way very different from that revealed by the printed word or fine art. Eaton was instructed in art and photography by his friend William Howes Hunt, a former linen draper, who lived in Great Yarmouth and there is great similarity in photographic subject and composition by them, both successful merchants. During the period 1848 - 55 Eaton records that his camera exposure times varied from 2½ to 15 minutes.

In the 1850s George Fitt and John Sawyer in Norwich were both very active using the new process of printing photographs from glass plate negatives and Henry Harmer continued to exhibit his work across the nation. In Edingthorpe, north Norfolk, the Reverend Joseph Sisson made photographs on glass (collodion positives) and published a booklet on the 'Turpentine-Waxed Paper Process'. It is evident that photography was

Hugh Diamond demonstrates printing.

well established in Norfolk by the 1850s and foreshadowed the rapid growth in its trade from then on.

W.J.J. Bolding – The Photographer

Photography emerged in western culture in 1839 and transformed our way of seeing, interpreting and remembering our world. During the next decade, enthusiastic gentlemen amateurs photographed family, friends, homes and local landscapes and WJJB was no exception. A wealthy landowner providing employment for many residents of Weybourne, he took to photography sometime during the 1840s and it is not known how he was taught. Dr. Hugh Diamond was both an active teacher and writer of photography and the photograph above shows Dr. Diamond in Norwich demonstrating printing to Thomas Mackinley and one of Thomas Eaton's sons.

Although there is no record, WJJB probably first used a tripod mounted, sliding box camera and, as designs improved, he surely upgraded as he felt necessary. During the 1840s, photographs were printed from paper or waxed paper negatives. These photographs (salted paper prints) had a soft, matt, painterly appearance but from the early 1850s glossy, high definition, monochrome photographs (albumen prints) were made from glass wet-plate negatives. WJJB used both processes and sometimes made albumen prints from wax-paper negatives. The wet-plate process was cumbersome and messy and negatives had to be developed in the dark while still wet. There came a time when WJJB decided to convert a barn for use as a studio and dark room and he greatly improved the lighting by installing very large windows as seen in the photograph opposite. When away from the studio, he had to take with him a dark tent and chemicals to develop the negatives.

In the studio WJJB eliminated any intrusive visual distractions by placing his sitters in front of a plain backdrop. Having previously exhibited paintings in public, WJJB's artistic eye undoubtedly informed what he saw in the inverted camera image under a dark cloth. His first family photographs, c. 1850, are examples of 'paper-on-paper' printing and they show his growing talent in enabling sitters to relax into his required composition. Children clearly trusted him and he was able to engage them in a variety of staged postures.

His exceptional talent is demonstrated with his decision to photograph his estate workers and Weybourne villagers in the 1850s and early 1860s. Almost all these portraits depict the sitters looking slightly away from the camera which sees them with a dignified eye. Many photographs are technically flawed by the inclusion of surface blemishes but are outstanding portraits of Norfolk rural workers in the mid-19th century and all the more memorable as he often shows them with the tools of their trades. No other photographer of this period in Norfolk is known to have achieved this and elsewhere in England such photographs were uncommon.

The north-facing window of WJJB's photographic studio.

1 **'The grieving mother'**. 1858

2 **'Lover of Literature'** This fine portrait, beautifully taken in natural light, shows Esther Monement in her mid-forties, eyes cast downwards to her left, while balancing a bound copy of the Cornhill Magazine, founded in 1860, on her lap. c1863.

3 **'The sleeping child'** 1858

4 Cicely Anne's grave in Weybourne churchyard

Post Mortem Images

Esther Monement with her daughter Cicely Anne, apparently asleep. The image is consistent with that of a loving mother holding her child but is, in fact, a post mortem photograph taken in 1858. It shows Esther in a most striking pose, sensitively captured by Bolding, revealing her dignity in this poignant moment. Dressed in mourning clothes, Esther is supporting her deceased daughter on her lap whilst her left index finger points upwards to heaven. The photograph provided a permanent reminder of her beloved child who died, just 16 months old. Other photographers might have added symbols of death such as a cut, wilting flower, a clock or a weeping willow, but Bolding chose simplicity. Against a plain background, this was probably taken in his studio at Weybourne.

Another photograph shows Cicely on a blanket in an artificially created 'natural' setting which includes harvested barley. It poses a conundrum; is she asleep or dead? At first glance it could be a picnic setting which gives the impression that she is asleep.

During this period, professional photographers exploited their opportunities by charging high prices for post mortem images as shown in this extract from an advertisement by J. Marchbank:

Remember! a good Likeness is all that can be rescued from the Grave.

How many have regretted, when it has been too late that they have not secured a resemblance of those who, by the tenderest ties of nature, are to them the dearest object on earth! With what tender emotion we can look at the Portrait of a dear departed friend! — and how it calls to mind their look, their words and their actions; affording therefore a consolation and pleasure not to be derived from any other earthly source!

Hannah Bolding had seven nieces. Here she is with one of them. Is it Cicely Anne? If so, then it is another 'Post Mortem' photograph.

The Second Eleven
photographs selected by John Benjafield

The Charming Niece. WJJB's charming niece Mary Esther Monement, aged about ten, dressed in a plain jacket with decorative edging and a wide brimmed hat. Looking slightly away from the camera, she is seen grasping a small bunch of cropped barley, the mainstay of WJJB's trade as a brewer.

The Hayricks. Two-wheeled carts, hayricks and a drying platform for straw in WJJB's fields. Made in the early 1850s, this is an important record of rural activity. The photographic paper is very thin and his hand written note suggests he was experimenting with 'albumenised paper' from a waxed paper negative and that 'varnishing it with gelatin made it better in many respects'. [WJJB's note reads 'These are all on albumenised paper Mur Bareytes 15 grains to 1 oz from a waxed paper neg taken at the same time as the other but with less sunshine. Make it better in many respects varnished with gelatine']

Melodramatics! These extraordinary images seem to show a woman, hands high in prayer, with a seated hidden figure and then the woman falling back from a ghostly stage apparition (opposite).

Sisters Reflecting. They are looking at their reflections. Hannah Beatrice Monement stands at the rear of this group, with her sister Mary Esther, seated and holding the mirror. The other girls are unidentified. c1863.

The Crow Scarer. Jon Tuck sits solidly in his working clothes, strong fingers clasped on his lap and his eyes firmly closed behind spectacles with their temple arms sunk into his bushy hair. He worked as a crow scarer, probably walking the fields using a wooden rattle. It is thought Tuck was a mariner who was given paid work by WJJB after he was saved from a shipwreck on the north Norfolk coast. c1855.

The Milk Boy. Billy came to collect milk from WJJB's farm every day. Here, WJJB has succeeded in getting Billy to sit holding his milk can while his legs dangle from the squab. Full-faced, his diet was surely wholesome. His well-worn, dusty boots suggest the daily trail he walked. c1855.

The Retired Sea Captain c1860.

The stern-looking Mr Allen. He is identified as 'A farmer from Cley'. Such is his expression, he could be just off to a funeral. Is he exceptionally tall or is the doorway very low? late 1860s. (Norfolk County Council).

Top and frontispiece:
The Watery Landscape.
WJJB occasionally ventured outside his studio with his camera and here he shows reeds and tall grasses in a pond with well-established trees on the bank. Given his interest in geology and archaeology, it may be a pingo pond. Pingos were earth mounds formed by pressure from ice beneath and when the ice melted the mounds collapsed, leaving depressions. They are found in north-west and south Norfolk.

Bottom: **The 'MUS' Bush.**
A group of bushes in a new plantation and to the left of the biggest is an upright quarry tile bearing the letters 'MUS'. In the background is WJJB's studio with two large window lights where most of his portraits were taken. c1855.

Chapter 3

Weybourne and the Bolding Family

The cliffs on the north-east coast of Norfolk, coming round from Yarmouth, reach a point where they taper off down to nothing, and to the west stretch sea level salt marshes for more than twenty miles towards Hunstanton.

Where cliffs end and sea level marshes begin, and a few hundred yards from the shoreline, sits the village of Weybourne. The locals pronounce it 'Web.urn' (said quickly), but since the beginning of time it has been through a wide variety of spellings.

The Holt/Cromer ridge of higher ground to the south of Weybourne was formed as a result of the deposits from the terminal moraine of the last Ice Age. On the downward slopes of the ridge, running north towards the sea, are a number of natural springs. These have fed and formed a stream (known as Spring Beck) since time immemorial which was a vital factor in the siting of a village settlement. Evidence of early occupation in the local area comes from the many prehistoric tumuli to be found along the ridge to the south (Salthouse and Kelling heaths), and finds of pottery, coins and other artefacts have indicated a strong presence from the Roman occupation in the early centuries of the first millennium.

William the Conqueror, after his victory at Hastings in 1066, granted the Lordship of Weybourne to a nephew, Hugh de Abrincis, Earl of Chester. In the 1086 Domesday Book the village was recorded with two mills (water-mills, fed by the natural stream) and was known as Wabrunna. Its origin has been suggested by Ekwall, in his classic book on the derivation of place-names, as coming from the Old English 'wearg-burna', the "felon stream" in which felons were drowned, a practice that continued in England in the Middle Ages well into the 15th century.

Wabrunne and Wayborn are other spellings of the village used in the Middle Ages, and the unlikely Wabornthorp in the early 18th century, but Wabourn, Waborn and Waborne are the common variations used during the 18th and 19th centuries. WJJB seems to have used 'Waborne' right through to the end of his life.

An important moment in the history of the village was the founding of an Augustinian priory in the reign of King John shortly after 1200, adjoining the parish church which had

Weybourne priory ruin. WJJB oil painting from the early 1850s

been started in the 11th century. Sir Ralph de Meyngaren, at that time Chief Justice of Chester, whose family had possessed the Manor (of Weybourne) as a subfeudary to the Earl of Chester since 1071, was made "Lord of the Town" and he and his wife Amicia founded the priory.

The Canons Regular of St Augustine, the Augustinian or Austin

Weybourne church and priory ruins today

'WJJB May 28 [18]50 Waborne Ch'. The priory ruins

Canons, who lived according to a Rule which had been derived from that drawn up by St Augustine, Bishop of Hippo in North Africa, in the 5th century, was an order which attempted to fill the gap that existed in the medieval church between the monk and the secular priest. Although they lived in the priory and were subject to the monastic rule, they went out to serve churches in the district as parish priests. The priory at Weybourne was endowed with the Church and Manor of Weybourne; in the course of time, through various grants, it held property in thirty Norfolk parishes. Its possessions, though widespread, were never extensive and throughout its life was in constant financial difficulties and nearly always understaffed. Shortly before the Dissolution of the Monasteries in the 1530s in Henry VIII's reign there was only a Prior and one Canon.

After the closure, the priory buildings, together with property in Weybourne and nearby villages, were granted to the Heydon and Gresham families, from whom they eventually passed to the Walpole family, who remain as Lords of the Manor and patrons of the parish church to this day. Through the centuries the priory ruins, with the parish church attached, have been the dominant architectural feature in the village, at the junction of the roads and a constant reminder of past history.

THE THREE MAPS - *opposite*

The author's mother-in-law was W.J.J.Bolding's great niece. In her house in Cley next the Sea, framed, was a copy of the 1586 map of the Cley and Blakeney Haven – a very fine map indeed, full of interesting historical/geographical detail. The whereabouts of the original is unknown. There are two other known copies of the same map. On a shelf in the cupboard below the gun cabinet in the same house, and rolled up, were the two other maps: the 1649 map of Salthouse, showing the village, the channel, the marshes and Van Haseduncks Bank of 1637; the 1704 map of Weybourne was a survey 'of the manor of Waybourne'. The 'town' is shown as divided into six parts with a road pattern very different from what we see today. Land ownership is clearly given, as well as the division of the fields into strips, as in medieval times, with the names given. It is a map of tremendous detail and interest.

I have always believed that the latter two maps were both originals.

A few years ago my brother-in-law deposited the three maps in the Norwich Record Office, where they would be available for study by people doing research. The experts at the Record Office analysed the maps and declared that they were all copies from the later 1840s. The writing on the maps was done by a metal pen nib, which was only in use from the middle of the 1840s, and not by a quill pen. That the two later maps were not originals came as a surprise, but excited me hugely. W.J.J.Bolding at that time was in his early thirties, and it is quite clear that he commissioned to have the copies made. He was that sort of person.

Right through to the 20th century the Manor Court and the Priory Court have dominated land holding in the village, a relic of the feudalism of the Middle Ages. By the 16th century the status of villein (unfree) tenants in the Manor had changed dramatically as a result of social and economic development. Tenure in villeinage had become a newly recognised secure form of tenure: tenure by 'copy' of the court roll 'at the will of the Lord according to the custom of the Manor'. Copyholders, as such tenants became known, derived their title from the details recorded on the Manorial Court Roll, of which they held a certified extracted 'copy'. By the 18th century, copyhold tenure could be freely bought and sold, mortgaged, sub-let and otherwise con-

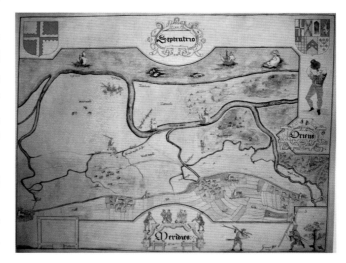

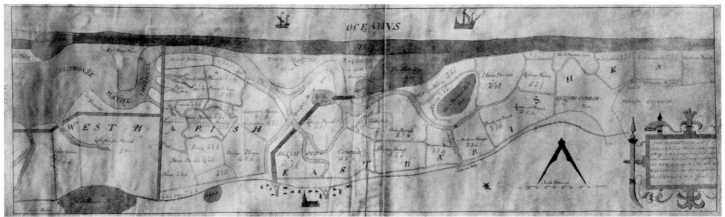

veyed, subject to the Manor Court and dependent on local custom. Upon a copyholder's death, his estate owed a heriot (fine – either, in earlier times, a best beast or a fixed sum of money) to the Lord of the Manor. The heir would appear

The 1586 map of Blakeney Haven and the port of Cley.

1649 map of Salthouse Marshes, showing Van Haseduncks Bank (1637) in the left centre and later Embankments (1649) on the left.

A close up of the centre of the village of Weybourne on the 1704 map. The house and 'bruery' acquired by William Jennis in 1748 are on the roadside, adjoining field number 149 belonging to Robert Brown.

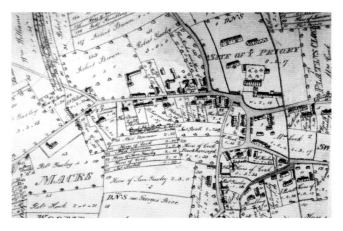

before the Manor Court and, following various rituals and customs, take possession of the land. By the end of the 19th century copyhold tenure was outdated and, by a series of Acts of Parliament, enfranchisement (turning copyhold into freehold with compensation) became the practice. It was not until the Law of Property Act in 1922 that all remaining copyhold land was to be converted into land of freehold tenure.

The sea has held great importance right through the story of Weybourne. Deep water immediately off shore has made it a potential landing place for invaders: the Angles, Saxons and Danes in early times, the threat of the Spanish towards the end of the 16th century, and in most recent times the threat of Hitler. Among the treasures at Hatfield House is a remarkable map from the 1580s of fortifications at Weybourne, stretching westwards from the end of the cliffs. In olden times Weybourne was a port, with a channel past Salthouse and then out to sea by the Cley Channel and Blakeney Harbour. In 1570 the village was credited with 4 ships and 17 mariners. Fishing and trade with foreign parts must have played a prominent part in the welfare of the village. The presence of a coastguard station by the beach at Weybourne shows how serious was the question of smuggling, an everyday occurrence along the whole stretch of coast.

The Jennis family were wealthy Yarmouth merchants from early times. A branch of the family purchased estates in north Norfolk and moved there by the early years of the 17th century, centred on the village of Sheringham (now Upper Sheringham). The church registers of that parish, during the 17th and 18th centuries, show a mass of Jennis baptisms, marriages and burials. The Waborne Manor Court Book from 1615 to 1655 has various entries relating to the family: 1615 Richard Jennys the Younger inherited land on the death of his father; 1648 Richard Jennys allowed his bakehouse and stable to be in decay; in 1655 Edmund and Samuel Jennys are mentioned. Then there is no entry until 1739 when Mary Jennis, spinster of Great Yarmouth, is recorded as a copyhold tenant. On 29th April 1686 in Sheringham church a William Jennis married; his wife Martha bore him twins in 1688, but on 7th January 1689 they were both buried. In 1696 another son, William, was born. He was the founder of the family 'dynasty' in Weybourne. It is now his fortunes that are considered through the scanty evidence.

Residing in Norwich, in the Norfolk Record Office, having come down through seven generations of the family, is the account book of the trading ship *William and Thomas*, registered at Blakeney but sailing mainly from Cley, which was owned by William Jennis, with him as master. Thirty-one voyages made between 1726 and 1733 are listed and the details make fascinating reading (see over). Twenty-six of the voyages were made in ballast to Newcastle to purchase coal for sale in north Norfolk. There were also two trips to Norway with 'freight',

'The House' (now the Maltings hotel, Weybourne) – WJJB's home for his whole life. Mid 1850s

two to London with barley, and one to Holland with a cargo of wool. Most of the voyages in the first few years recorded made a profit, but by the close of the 1720s the majority were making a loss. The end came with the vessel most likely either being laid up or being sold.

8th November 1748 was a momentous day, because that was when 'William Jennis, mariner, of Upper Sheringham, on the surrender of William Cooke of Suffield' purchased copyhold, through the Waborne Manor Court, sixty-nine acres with a house and 'bruery', with a fine of £25. 4. 0 paid to the Lord of the Manor. He was the great great grandfather of WJJB, so the wheels of inheritance were now set in motion. A number of personalised blue-and-white plates from a dinner service survive, dated 1749: 'William Jenis of Wabon in C Sorfolk' (did the engraver of the plates interpret an 'N' as 'CS'?). The indications are that the plates were made in Holland; three fish 'swim' within the pattern, supporting William Jennis's strong association with the sea. The last piece of evidence surviving is a beautifully written statement of account for the sum of one shilling and sixpence. It is dated 1765, the year before William Jennis died, and is from Richard Girdlestone, Deputy Searcher in the Ports of Blakeney and Cley. His fee was for checking nine lasts of malt (one last equals eighty bushels – a dry measure of 640 gallons) into a vessel called

September y 23 day 1726

	£	s	d
Saled for new castell of y forth vige in y ss Thomas of Blakley ff Jennies murster and acornts of y disparments			
for y vige paid for 12 steren of beef	05	11	8
paid for twee barell of bare	00	16	0
paid for 9 stone of brade	00	08	0
october paid for half bushell of beef	00	02	0
y 14 day paid for y ½ stone of beefe	05	11	9
paid for half hundred of brade	00	17	8
paid for half barell of beeare	00	04	—
paid for y pilet goe out and tides worke	00	10	0
october paid for 2 stone of sale	00	02	8
y 29 day paid for ss stone of beef	05	05	8
at newcast paid for hundred wight of breade	00	09	0
paid for one barell of bare	00	08	0
paid for twentey porre of candel	00	08	0
paid for a hought for a warter caste	00	03	0
paid for 3 stone of robe	00	03	6
paid for new feares	00	01	8
paid for y Gales at newcastl	00	16	0
paid for ss pounde of chies	00	02	2
paid for 24 cholder of coals at 10 s chold at	12	12	7
mor for kil dues	00	19	
paid for 30 cholder of Cinders at newcastel	18	00	00
paid for y trining of y coals & Cinders	00	08	0
paid for twee new showels & mendiny	00	12	6
paid for y claring at y coustores at newcast	01	18	4
paid for y rowen hores at newcastel	00	19	0
paid for a booket and for y boost	00	02	8
paid for a boole to roue ill and out	00	04	6
	38	07	9

november ye 7 day 1726

	li	s	d
Rived of Glashey from newcastel of ye forth vige paid for ye pilot came in	00	6	0
paid for tides workes — — — — —	00	7	0
paid to fower men wages for ye vige	00	5	0
paid to ye boye for his vige —	00	13	0
for my selfe — — — — —	03	00	0
paid to 4 men for haven of 17 chold of coal	00	04	6
paid for ye Lighter oure of 36 chold of coal	00	18	0
paid for 3 men livering of 40 out of ship	00	10	0
paid for harber dues & kee dues —	00	13	4
paid for Loveing at ely — — —	00	06	0
paid for 40 3/4 of couls & cinders the Dutey 20	00	02	8
paid for ye Retreven at ye coshore	00	02	4
	37	12	10
	38	07	00
	75	19	00
Credor for uphold^r of couls at afor a chold	56	13	00
Credor for 19 choldur of cinders at 05–05 a chold	30	09	00
— in all —	87	02	00
	75	19	00
cleard —	95	02	03

wm Hopkins

SIR JOHN FENN (1739–94) – ANTIQUARY

John Fenn was the son of a surgeon. After education at grammar school in Norfolk and north Suffolk, he went up to Caius College, Cambridge. While there he met John Frere, whose sister Ellenor he courted, and then married on 1st January 1766. The newly-weds went to live in Dereham, Norfolk (their house is now the Hill House Hotel), a fine Georgian brick mansion. They had no children, but brought up an orphaned heiress and later their nephew William Frere. Between 1768 and 1775 Fenn helped William Whittingham to publish the remaining parts of Francis Blomefield's *History of Norfolk*. In the mid 1770s he acquired the Paston Letters, the correspondance of the Paston family between 1422 and 1509. They give an important insight into the lives and political intrigues of well off people at the end of the medieval period.

Fenn collected together the letters, edited them and then published them. In January 1787 the first two volumes appeared, and were dedicated to his monarch, George III. In May of that year Fenn presented the originals to the king, and received a knighthood. In 1789 a third and fourth volume were published. Work on a final volume of letters was put on hold when Fenn was appointed High Sheriff of Norfolk in 1791, and wasn't completed when he died in February 1794. He was buried with his wife at the Frere family church of St Bartolomew, Finningham in Suffolk.

There was erected a marble monument to them by John Bacon, sculptor (1740–99).

the *Edward and Ann* of Cley. The malt was to be shipped to Rotterdam.

William Jennis in 1717 had married Elizabeth Martha Fenn (Sir John Fenn was a descendant of hers). Her family were also originally from Yarmouth, where they had been prominent citizens since the Middle Ages, but at the end of the 17th century a branch had moved to Sheringham. William and Elizabeth did not have a son, but a daughter Martha (1718-51). She married Nicholas Bolding (1708-41) whose family can be traced back to the 1660s in Sheringham. The young Boldings lived at Edgefield near Holt, only a few miles from Weybourne, in 'a long, low house with six or eight windows at the front and an avenue of trees leading to it.' A son William (1736-1801) was born. At the age of fifteen he was orphaned, becoming the responsibility of his widower grandfather William Jennis for his upbringing, and the heir to the Jennis inheritance. This was proven at the sitting of the Waborne Manor Court on 7th December 1767 when he was admitted under the will of William Jennis who died in 1766.

At the time of his grandfather's death, William Bolding was married with two children: Ann Bolding (1760-1823) and William Bolding (1761-1813). Father and son having the same christian name has caused confusion because it has been difficult to distinguish between them in family correspondence at the end of the 18th century. William's wife Elizabeth (*nee* Platten) bore him five more children: Elizabeth Jennis Bolding (1768-1858), Mary Bolding (1769-1810) who married Augustine Spaul from a seafaring Blakeney family, Sarah Bolding (1772-1824), Margaret Bolding (1775-1827) and John Bolding (1780-1847) who married Esther Johnson (1790-1868) of Cley. They were the parents of WJJB.

The two brothers William and John were nineteen years apart in age. William never married and one gets the picture that his much younger brother John was very much an 'apprentice' waiting in the wings. The strong family connection with the sea continued. A series of letters from Captain Augustine Spaul survive, which show some insight into events from further afield. Spaul was sailing between English and Dutch ports and he usually brought back presents for the family. In one letter from an eleven year old John Bolding (1791) he is asked to bring back 'a butt of currants for mother and two clever young men as husbands for my sisters.' In a later letter Spaul wrote from Bristol to say that he would sail on the next tide for Lynn. He would come close to Weybourne and when he could see the house he would hoist his ensign and fire a gun. All these ships were armed to protect themselves from the French. An extract from one of his letters reads, 'This is to inform you of my safe arrival at Liverpool after an indifferent passage from Blakeney. We had the hardest gale that I was ever in, which blew us down the coast of France, but the weather coming fine we got clear and have everything in order again with very little damage....I could wish to be at home for Cley Fair but do not expect to return till November.'

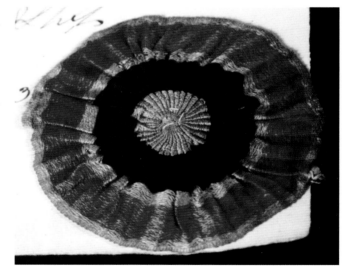

In the early days of the French Revolution, Spaul had taken a cargo of grain to a very hungry port on the River Seine. The delighted people presented him with one of their red, white and blue emblems. This was when these colours were first adopted by the supporters of the Revolution. The cockade survives in the family to this day. Not long after this voyage the French Convention declared war on Britain. This upset the pattern of trade for some of the vessels which sailed from Blakeney.

The cockade given, in appreciation, to Augustine Spaul when he arrived with a cargo of grain at a port on the River Seine in the early days of the French Revolution – early 1790s

A drawing by John Bolding, dating from the 1790s, found in the family collection

John Bolding, when in his middle teens, went to sea with his brother-in-law to see if he could take to a life at sea. Captain Spaul's ship was then trading up and down the English coast, collecting coal from Newcastle to bring south, taking wheat from Norfolk to London and elsewhere. How long John Bolding's seafaring experience lasted is not clear, but a letter from his sister Mary indicates that he was now 'not quite so fond of it as he was' and not long after he confirmed his sister's impression that he felt he was not cut out to be a sailor, but would agree to do it if the family could find no other suitable occupation for him. Anyway, he gave up the life of a young mariner to start learning the family business from his father and then his elder brother. Luckily he was ashore by the time he was eighteen, because the *Norwich Mercury* of 10th November 1798 recorded that 'The *Elizabeth* of Blakeney, Austin Spaul master, laden with coal for Rochester, was driven ashore at Horsy in Norfolk; the master was forced off the deck by the violence of the sea, and unfortunately drowned.' He is buried in Blakeney churchyard.

A series of letters survive, from Captain Harrison to John Bolding, from the years 1806-10. As young men the two had been together on a family ship a decade before and had become firm friends. Harrison's letters to John give details of the Napoleonic wars. In October 1805 the French fleet had been destroyed at Trafalgar and the fear of a landing on the Norfolk coast faded away. It was now safer to trade further afield. In 1807 Harrison sailed from Lynn to the Baltic, where he had trouble with ice, and later in the same year he was at the Russian port of Onega in the White Sea. The Peninsular War started in 1808 and Harrison and his Blakeney ship was on military transport service. In one letter to John he reported that on his return from Lisbon to Portsmouth he was ordered to Ramsgate, there to embark thirty-four horses of the 12th Light Dragoons. He should have taken them to Antwerp but could not get up the river because Flushing had not surrendered when he got there.

Napoleon with a large army was advancing through Spain; his aims included the capture of Lisbon. However, a small force under Sir John Moore, immortalised in Charles Wolfe's poem, cut the French supply route, whereupon Napoleon turned on them. This saved Lisbon. The British withdrew to the port of Corunna with a superior French army in pursuit. Harrison's vessel was one of those sent to evacuate the British troops. An extract from his letter of February 1809 reads:

> Such a scene of misery and confusion God grant that I may never see again. I was within one-and-half miles of the Battle of Corunna and saw both Sir John Moore and Sir David Bard brought off the field. Towards evening it got very thick and duskey. We could not see that part of the engagement where our people charged the enemy up the hill. The French had great advantage in numbers and position on the hill but still we made them run. The miserable objects that were wounded were shocking sights. War is a most dreadful thing. Happy England that only hears of such things without witnessing them.

One indication of the family status in Weybourne at the beginning of the 19th century is shown in the Inclosure Award of 1805 for Waborne. The Lord of the Manor, Lord Walpole, was by far the biggest landowner. William Bolding was one of a number of smaller landowners who appealed at the Norfolk Sessions against Lord Walpole 'in respect of the right of fold course or the liberty of sheepwalk called the Waborne sheep-walk'. Not an isolated case with Inclosure nationally of a big landowner trying to cream off rights for himself. William Bolding owning under fifty acres and renting a further seventy-six acres appears to be the fifth biggest landowner in the parish.

The 1748 deed bringing William Jennis to Weybourne had mentioned a 'bruery'. Shortly before his death, William Bolding bought three public houses: The Crown and Anchor and The Ship, both in his home village, and The Chequers at Gresham. These purchases seem to indicate the beginning of the serious building up of the Weybourne Brewery and the

The Valentine, certainly John Bolding's own work, sent by him in 1809 to Esther Johnson of Cley next the Sea. He married her in 1814 in Cley church.

family extending their public house properties in north Norfolk. William died in 1813 and it was now that his much younger sibling John 'came of age' (aged 33) and inherited the family estates.

At this time John Bolding was unmarried, but he was courting a girl from Cley next the Sea, Esther Johnson, and had been for a number of years. An outstanding hand-coloured Valentine sent by John to Esther in 1809 survives:

Sure, as the grapes grow on the vine
I choose you for my Valentine
The rose is red the violet blue
Carnations sweet and so are you
Accept these lines that here are pen'd
Without offence from a true friend
And should kind fortune be my lot
Some day may tie the wedding knot

John and Esther were married in Cley church in 1814. Esther had grown up in Cley and branches of the Johnson family had extensive small land holdings in north Norfolk. Esther's father William Johnson (1750-1814) had married Hannah Smith (1756-1837) who was from Wiveton, where her family owned land. Esther's younger brother John Francis Johnson (1798-1844) later farmed in Salthouse and lived at the Manor Farmhouse below the church. Their parents retired to Salthouse and both are buried in the nave aisle of that fine church. Parcels of Johnson and Smith land in Cley, Wiveton and elsewhere became absorbed into the Bolding 'empire' in the course of time.

William Johnson Jennis (WJJB) was born in 1815, destined not to marry and to live in the family home, 'The House' in the middle of Weybourne, for the whole of his life. In 1816 a sister Hannah Elizabeth was born, also not to marry, and to live with her brother until her death in 1892. In 1819 Mary Ann was born, but she died the following year. A third sister

Esther ('Young' Esther) was born in 1820, destined to marry William Monement of King's Lynn, to be the mother of eleven children, and to die in 1871 at the age of fifty-one. It is this family that were to play a pivotal role in the photographic reputation of WJJB. A last sister Sarah Ann was born in 1826, but she failed to survive beyond a young age, dying in 1831 when WJJB was fifteen.

John Bolding was quite clearly a clever, astute businessman, an entrepreneur in modern language. During the 1820s he was steadily buying up properties and land, including five public houses in north Norfolk (at Wells-next-the-Sea, Sheringham, Holt, Cley and Overstrand); almost nothing in the 1830s, but in 1842 no less than five more public houses (at Aylsham, Cromer, Sheringham, Thurgarton and Edgefield). The 1841 Tithe apportionment records John Bolding owning 173 acres of land, renting another 20 acres from Robert Hammond, and owning a further eleven cottages and gardens. This shows how the family fortunes had progressed since the beginning of the century at the time of Inclosure. He was now the largest resident landowner in the village. (The absentee Lord of the Manor, the Earl of Orford, owned 1320 acres.) Later that year the watermill at Weybourne was purchased from Thomas Armes, with a corn postmill on a plot of land adjacent. In *White's Gazetteer and Directory of Norfolk* for 1845 John Bolding Esq. is listed as 'brewer and maltster'. This raises two

The mill pond for WJJB's watermill in Weybourne, with his postmill behind. A brown wash drawing from the late 1840s.

WJJB's postmill looking rather dilapidated with only two sails – 1880s, quite likely taken by WJJB's niece Rose Monement. There has been no evidence of this mill above ground for over a hundred years.

points. Firstly, the 'Esq.' signifies Bolding as a gentleman, rather than just as a 'merchant', when he would be middle class, but still possibly of yeoman stock. Secondly, 'brewer and maltster' indicates that the brewing part of the family enterprise was most likely extremely profitable at certain times, enabling him to invest in property. The 1841 census, the first to give clear details of residents in households, has John Bolding and his wife Esther, his three surviving children, now all grown up, three male servants, two aged 20 and one 15, and three female servants, one aged 20 and two aged 15. The family were indeed comfortably off.

WJJB must have been seated in front of the entrance to the House when executing this pencil drawing from the 1840s of the wrought iron gate and fences which marked WJJB's properties on either side of the village street (compare with the brown wash drawing of the House on page 46). The extent of the formal garden, which extended round the back of the Cottage, can be clearly seen.

Chapter 4

William Johnson Jennis Bolding

(1815-99)

Landowner, Farmer, Brewer, Maltster, multiple Public House Owner, Publican, Bottle Manufacturer, Ship Owner. Then his extra mural activities: Artist, Silhouettist, Etcher, Photographer, Archaeologist, Geologist, Scientist, Naturalist, Botanist, Gardener, Wood Turner. Add to this, given to me by an octogenarian descendant of WJJB's living in Weybourne: Taxidermist, Jewellery Maker, Stone Polisher. A truly remarkable and extraordinarily able human being.

Nothing whatsoever is known about WJJB's academic education. How big an influence was his father? Was he tutored at home? Did he go away to school somewhere? As with so much of his life, it is questions being asked with very few answers being given. Snippets of information on the family in these years are few and far between. In October 1823 'Old' Esther and her children were staying at her old home in Cley when a note arrived by hand. It was from her exhausted and obviously shaken husband John back in Weybourne:

Oil painting of W.J.J.Bolding by an unknown artist. His stock and pronounced sloping shoulder line were the height of fashion in the late 1830s. This would put him around the age of twenty-five.

WJJB's brown wash drawing. c1845 of 'The House', his home for the whole of his life. Since being sold out of the family in 1946 it has been a hotel: the Maltings hotel.

A view of the Maltings hotel. c1995.

Oct. 30, 1823 Weyborn

Ship ashore

I am sorry to inform you that I witnessed a shocking shipwreck. A brig from Naples bound for Hull came ashore at Sparrow gap. Richard Johnson and myself were the only two at her when she struck. One of the men jumped overboard and after running in two or three times I succeeded in getting him safe ashore. The master jumped almost at the same time and I got close to him once but I am sorry to say that he went round the stern. I followed him along the beach but poor fellow I saw him go down among the breakers. Six men were saved. Tell Mr Jackson the brig was laden with olive oil and in large pipes, a very valuable cargo. The ship was all to pieces soon after the men were out and the cash (boxes or crates) was all floating to Salthouse and Clay.*

• Clay (Claye) was the spelling on maps from the 16th century. 'Cley' began to be used from the middle of the 18th century, and became the standard spelling by the middle of the 19th century onwards.

Six years later, WJJB's younger sister Esther, when she was nine years old, wrote some verses after another shipwreck off the Weybourne beach:

Lines written on a vessel, wrecked at Weybourne on 14th October 1829 in which all hands were lost.

The storm is high, the billows rise,
And dash the Ships upon the shore,
The Sailors now with watery eyes
Lament those friends they see no more.

Alas! Alas! They all must die,
For none of them can reach the shore,
Nor can they from the billows fly,
For ah! They sink to rise no more.

For the Amighty's word is given,
And they are buried in the deep,
But they will meet their God in Heaven,
Where they will have no more to weep

Esther – aged 9 years

The *Norfolk Chronicle* for Saturday 17th October 1829 recorded the event in brutal detail, 'CROMER – 14th October: A gale of wind from the N.E. Began to blow early this morning and raging with great violence throughout the day continues unabated to this hour (7 p.m.) ... an unfortunate Billy-boy (a sloop rigged barge so named) which had passed this place (Cromer) in the course of the afternoon, to the northward. Off Wayborn this little vessel encountered a heavy sea, which after washing every man overboard, capsised and knocked her to pieces: all hands perished.'

In old age WJJB acknowledged 1830, when he was in his fifteenth year, as being the date from which he started studying the archaeology of his parish church with its extensive medieval priory ruins. This was to be a lifetime fascination and sixty years on he was probably the leading authority on its interpretation.

It is with WJJB's art and a date of 1832 that factual information can be gleaned, and from it strong suppositions can possibly be made. The draw-

Pencil drawing of 'Cley Church, Norfolk' inscribed WJJB and dated 1832 when he was seventeen years old. His mother Esther was born and brought up in Cley until her marriage to John Bolding in 1814.

A pencil drawing by WJJB from the 1830s of St George and the Dragon, one of the corbels supporting the niches above the pillars in Cley church.

ing in question, done in pencil, is of Cley church, executed from the north-west. This is the church of his mother's home village and the one in which his parents were married.

What is remarkable about this drawing, apart from its quality, is that it is an almost exact copy of the John Berney Ladbrooke lithograph printed in 1824. In the 1820s Robert Ladbrooke (1769-1842), a contemporary and relation by marriage of John Crome (1768-1821), the founder of the Norwich School of Artists, set out to draw every church in Norfolk, six hundred and sixty-seven of them, and his son John Berney Ladbrooke (1803-79) helped him and produced some of the lithographs. In the early 1820s the younger Ladbrooke was working in London where he twice exhibited at the Royal Academy. He started giving drawing lessons from this time. Back in Norfolk he was based in Norwich but was prepared to travel 'to attend Private Families or schools contiguous to the line through which he passes' (*Norwich Mercury*, 23 January 1836). Sidney D.Kitson, in his 1937 biography of John Sell Cotman, had written that 'at this time (c1800), and indeed for the next forty years or more, the accepted method of learning was to copy the original work of a professional artist'. That John Berney Ladbrooke was a drawing master to the sixteen-year-old WJJB was quite possible, and to draw Cley church was an obvious choice for the gifted pupil. It has been put to me more recently, by an expert on the Norwich School, that it is just as likely that WJJB will have been self taught with his art, as this was not unusual at that time in the 19th century for the offspring of well-to-do families. Also dated 1832 are a series of architectural pencil drawings from West Norfolk, loose in a folder. Such places as Great Massingham church, the font in Old Hunstanton church, Terrington St Clement church and St Margaret's church in King's Lynn were drawn.

Three brown wash drawings heightened with white on brown paper, all clearly from the same period, are stuck in a wonderful album of WJJB's artwork. One of the drawings is signed and dated 1833. It has a strong Dutch windmill with water

From a small sketchbook of drawings in West Norfolk all dated 1833: 'font Hunstanton church from a very slight sketch' grey wash.

look about it. A second is of Barnard Castle which generates great atmosphere. The third is remarkably different. It is of the tomb of General Foy (Maximilien Sebastian Foy) (1775-1825) in the Cimitiere du Pere Lachaise, Paris. Foy was a French general under Napoleon Bonaparte and commanded a division of infantry at the battle of Waterloo in 1815, in which he received his fifteenth wound. This terminated his military career. (God Bless Google and Wikipedia which gave me a photograph of the tomb and career details of Foy in under one minute.) These three drawings were quite clearly part of WJJB's artistic education and he will have copied them from original works (see over).

WJJB's younger sister Hannah had a dramatic and frightening experience in 1833 or thereabouts. She was driving her trap along the coast road near Morston when she had a brush with smugglers. A man dashed out into the road, took the pony's head and turned the trap into a field. Hannah was threatened and told to stay in the field, but she did see a line of men with donkeys heading inland. When released she made for home at a good pace.

Smuggling was clearly very active along the Norfolk coast from early times and up to and including the 19th century. The Coast Guard Station,

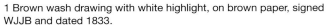

1 Brown wash drawing with white highlight, on brown paper, signed WJJB and dated 1833.

2 'Barnard Castle, Durham' – brown wash drawing with white highlight on brown paper. c1833.

3 The tomb of General Maximilien Foy in the Cimitiere du Pere Lachaise, Paris. Brown wash drawing with white highlight on brown paper. c1833.

by the beach at Weybourne, was fully manned, and on occasions had to deal with violent situations, as the example printed opposite from a newspaper of the time shows:

CLEY, Feb. 28 (1833)

Desperate affray with and capture of smugglers

On the morning of Tuesday last, about half-past one o'clock, a most desperate affray took place between Lieut. George Howes, Royal Navy, Chief Officer of the Coast Guard Station at Weybourne, assisted by part of his crew, against a large party of armed smugglers, who resisted the officers in taking a quantity of contraband goods, which had been landed on the beach at Kelling, in this county; Lieut. Howes and crew were obliged to fire on the party several times in self defence, and succeeded in taking two men, with five horses, and six carts laden with brandy and tobacco; (when the landing was first seen twenty-three carts were sighted); one of the men taken was so desperately wounded in the legs from a shot he received, that surgical assistance was rendered him immediately on his arrival here (Cley), he was obliged to have one leg amputated; the other man was very slightly wounded in the face, and we are given to understand several that escaped were very much injured in the affray. The quantity of goods taken in the carts and on the beach was 127 half ankers (= 550 gallons) of brandy and between three and four thousand pounds of manufactured tobacco, which are all safely lodged in his Majesty's Custom House Warehouse at this port (Cley); too much praise cannot be given to Lieut. Howes for his exertions in the above affair.

I have found a reference concerning WJJB and smuggling, the source of which I am unable to pinpoint. 'It is reputed that he turned a blind eye to smuggled goods landed on the beaches bordering his property and was duly rewarded with a couple of tubs left discreetly on his doorstep.' Back in the 18th century, when smuggling was endemic, Parson Woodforde, Rector of Weston Longville near Norwich, openly accepted smuggled goods, and his diary for 29th March 1777 recorded: 'Andrews the Smuggler brought me this night about 11 o'clock a bagg of Hyson Tea 6 Pd weight. He frightened us a little by whistling under the Parlour Window just as we were going to bed. I gave him some Geneva and paid him for the tea at 10/6 per Pd 3. 3. 0.' By WJJB's day, at the time of his father's

Pencil drawing, signed H.S.B, from about 1835, inscribed on the back 'Miss Esther Bolding with Sophia's love'. Esther was WJJB's younger sister, later to marry William Monement and to be the mother of eleven children.

death in 1847, smuggling on the Norfolk coast, and all through the kingdom, was much reduced. In the 1840s Britain entered a period of free trade. Tariffs on most goods were greatly reduced, or were abolished altogether. This made the risks of smuggling too great, and support for smugglers weakened.

If only 'Young' Esther's journal still existed, my life would be so much easier. A number of details from it were used by Derick Mellor in his articles in the 1970s on the family in *Norfolk Fair*. Esther most likely kept her journal during her teenage years and up to her marriage, and probably for a year or two beyond. We are given an insight into everyday life at home in Weybourne in the 1830s and 1840s.

Esther intended to marry when the right man turned up and she was not averse to learning the household arts of those days. Pickling samphire had more appeal than some because it could be combined with a picnic when the green shoots were ready for picking on the marshes in May. Another favourite was making mead; sweet briar, thyme and bay leaves had to be prepared with mace and other spices; the household notes about mead refer to using thirty pounds of honey! A happy note written one Sunday morning, records how she had made a Simnel-cake as a surprise for her mother; on top were eleven sugar birds' eggs because this was the eleventh month of the church year. On this Sunday Esther intended to visit her aunt at Salthouse and take sugar-cakes for the children whom she adored.

Esther recorded in her journal that William (WJJB) usually went away in May with his fishing gear and sketching things. One year the journal states that he was at Tintern Abbey on the Wye (see page 55), but very little of his artistic output from c1835 to his father's death in 1847 seems to have survived.

When WJJB was away then, their mother invited young friends to stay. One was Captain Edward Taylor, who had been mate of one of the family ships and was now with the East India Company. Esther records her

A peaceful corner of WJJB's garden with two bee hives. (Norfolk County Council)

THE MANOR HOUSE, SALTHOUSE – AND THE JOHNSON FAMILY

The Manor House, Salthouse

William Johnson and his wife Hannah acquired the Manor House and Manor Farm in 1796 and they moved from Cley. After the Purdys, they were the leading residents in Salthouse. It was their daughter Esther who married John Bolding of Weybourne in 1814 in Cley church. They were the parents of W.J.J.Bolding. On a slab in the central aisle of the nave in Salthouse church, William (died 1814) and Hannah (died 1837) are commemorated. Their son John Francis Johnson, born 1798, in time lived in the Manor House with his wife Elizabeth, and his brother-in-law John Bolding helped him with his farming. In 1844 John Francis Johnson died leaving a six-year-old son William (1838-75), and it was W.J.J.Bolding who now was responsible for looking after the farming affairs of his young cousin. The pencil drawing of the Manor House by Bolding was executed on one of his visits to Salthouse, probably about 1850.

Young William Johnson clearly grew up to be a troubled young man. In 1869 he married a village girl, Sarah Pigott, but by 1875 he had drunk himself to death. Sarah was now owner of the Manor House and farm, but she proceeded to split up the farm among many tenants (her relations). She lived on in the Manor House until her death in 1909.

Sir Christopher Myngs (1625-66), one of three Norfolk born English admirals of the 17th century, was probably born in the Manor House. The other two admirals were Sir John Narborough (c1640-88) and Sir Cloudesley Shovell (1650-1707).

views in clear and careful handwriting: 'How very much he is improved. There is so much quiet and unassuming frankness in his manner, so very good natured and free of conceit. He has brought a great number of gifts from India and China, more than he ought. There is no life like a sailor's, none that produces so much manliness of purpose, such courage and indifference to hardship. He has left off smoking as he thinks it makes a man weak and nervous. He was saying why English sailors were much the best, because the more dangers an Englishman encounters the cooler and more collected he becomes.'

A watercolour 'Tintern' – Tintern Abbey on the Welsh bank of the River Wye in Monmouthshire. c1840.

Edward was pressed into helping with the rustic sports in the village. The journal states that Esther's father usually provided a pig for the roasting and the girls gave much thought to their dresses. The day included, among other events, a donkey race, a grinning competition and dipping for eels.

WJJB's name as purchaser on a property in Weybourne is first recorded in 1839 when he was twenty-four; in 1840 two Weybourne properties and in 1841 the Calthorpe Arms in Blakeney. He was being groomed to take over the family businesses. His father in 1840 was sixty years old.

It is almost certainly 1844 that WJJB and his sisters went to Yorkshire to visit the Ingham family. There is no mention of the parents travelling, so this, for WJJB, will have been a business trip as Bolding ships carried Mr Ingham's coal to King's Lynn, north Norfolk and further afield. Derick Mellor in one of his articles wrote that 'they returned to Norfolk in time for the corn harvest and that Esther was married before the next harvest came round'. They travelled by coach to Lynn, then by sea to Hull. The journal gives a wonderful descriptive account of the voyage.

On board the *Albatross* we sailed about five in the afternoon and after a not very pleasant passage we reached Hull at six in the morning. There were a great many passengers on board; one little deaf and dumb boy going to the Manchester school interested me more than any. We obtained places on the sofa but I could not sleep. After passing Spurn light it was smooth water. At Hull there were many vessels, much larger than I had seen before, with a forest of masts and sail, and there was one miserable steamer but I have no taste for them. We left by train for Dewsbury; I can scarcely describe my sensations travelling by railway, the immense deal of preparation, the long train of carriages and an engine belching smoke. At first it makes you feel that it is something rather awful, but that feeling soon wears away and you can scarcely believe you are going with such velocity, they say 37 miles to the hour.

The Boldings stayed with the Inghams at Blake Hall near Wakefield for two weeks. They made a visit to Mr Ingham's coal mines. The girls said they did not want to go down the pit after their six mile walk over the moors. The journal refers to a colossal winding engine and the little carts on a railroad which conveyed the coal. The opinion was that to work in a mine would be eternal death.

They also visited York. 'At the great Minster the guide somewhat spoiled our feelings and reflection in this place of great beauty.' Esther wished she had been able to stay for divine service. They visited Clifford's Tower which was surrounded by the massive stone buildings of the prison. 'There were a great number of prisoners awaiting deportation, distinguished by their blue-and-white dress. The cells are formed of four whole stones of immense size, double-barred windows and an iron door.' While in York WJJB was able to obtain a sickle made for a left-handed man on the farm and light ones for women working in the harvest fields.

This visit to Yorkshire was to end with a week up at Otley. The journal gives a detailed account of this visit:

Tuesday, left Blake Hall feeling quite vexed at having to part from such kind people and particularly from little Emily. We took the train to Leeds. I have quite decided I do not like the railway; it saves time but there is not the excitement of travelling fast with a horse and the noise is most disagreeable. Hannah and I took a fly from Leeds and as we neared Otley the beauty of the Yorkshire scenery burst upon us. It was really splendid, beautiful beyond description. I hope that

1 William and Mary Monement. c1855. This is an historically important photograph. They were both born in the 1770s and were over the age of sixty when photography was first invented.

2 A splendid composition photograph of William Monement (senior). c1856.

3 William Monement (senior). c1857.

4 Mary Monement (1777-1869). c1855.

Miniature watercolour, by an unknown artist, to celebrate the engagement of Esther Bolding and William Monement in 1844.

William can capture this beauty in his painting.

The account continues:

... many very merry walks over the moors and two rather grim visits to the mills. The cotton mill had an immense deal of machinery all worked by a tremendous water-wheel; there were two hundred looms in one room and the noise was deafening. The other visit was to a worstead mill making a kind of Orleans cloth. Mr Ingham observed that if only Norfolk had some rivers which could provide water-power then we would still have a textile industry and prosperity, but now our people are driven to take passage to Australia where there is the farm work they understand.

A delightful miniature watercolour portrait of Esther and William Monement survives, celebrating their engagement. Their marriage took place on 27th August 1845 in Weybourne church. William Monement by this time must have been prominent in his family's business in King's Lynn. In the 1845 edition of *White's Directory of Norfolk* two cork cutters and merchants were trading in Lynn, one of them Monement and Son, 79 Norfolk Street. He was the 'Son'. His father, also William (1779-1858), was close to retirement. The Monement family must originally have come from the Low Countries, of Huguenot stock, forced across from the continent in the 16th century as a result of the Catholic persecutions of Protestants. I have found mention on Google of a Monement in the Fakenham area of Norfolk towards the end of the 16th century. The older William Monement grew up at Sculthorpe near Fakenham, before setting up in business in Lynn.

The Monement newly weds went to live in Lynn, above the business

Four silhouettes by WJJB
(about twenty survive). Hannah
Johnson (1840-1925) (top left)
was the daughter of John
Francis Johnson (1798-1846) of
the Manor House, Salthouse.
This silhouette dates from
about 1845. The sitters in all
the others are unknown, but I
wonder if one of these two men
might be WJJB's father John
Bolding who died in 1847
before his son became involved
in taking photographs.

premises in Norfolk Street; this was a huge change for Esther who had been brought up in a coastal village where farming, brewing, fishing and fish-curing were almost the only occupations. They kept returning for visits to Weybourne, which they continued to do for the rest of Esther's life. The first visit back to north Norfolk after their wedding was for Esther's birthday in October; the journal was still going, and we read that the mud was already deep on parts of the highway. Her father was far from well and worrying about small things. Someone had dug a ditch, to divert water from the beck although the Manor Court had long before established that only the fish-house could have a channel from this stream on which the corn-mill depended. Again, the old man was annoyed because no one had taken down the sparrow-pots until the sparrow population had increased enormously. In any case he could no longer enjoy sparrow pie.

The journal, at this time, recorded that one of the family ships, the *Camellia*, a 72 ton schooner, was in Blakeney harbour to make up the annual accounts. The two Bolding sisters each had an eighth share in the vessel. Charles Temple, a Blakeney merchant, owned half (thirty-two shares) and a Blakeney fisherman and another merchant each had eight shares. The *Camellia* had been built at Hull in 1838 and the Bolding sisters ownership is recorded on 21st December of that year when the ship put in to the harbour at Wells-next-the-Sea. The same port shipping register recorded the vessel on 9th May 1861 with the two sisters still as owners. One last reference is found in R & B Larn's *Shipwreck Index* where the *Camellia* is shown to have been wrecked off Blakeney on 19th January 1881 en route from Great Yarmouth: 'vessel stranded and lost in wind conditions E force 10'. Nothing is stated whether there was loss of life. Searches through the Norfolk newspapers found no mention of the *Camellia*, but a number of reports of atrocious weather conditions all round the Norfolk coast at that time. WJJB, as stated in the journal, was given something for his museum; it was an eyebolt which had been taken from the wreck of the *Bounty*. Captain Ashley who presented it had prepared a little book with the narrative; this included impressions on visiting Pitcairn Island where lived the descendants of the mutineers and the native women whom they had taken with them. 'The young women were objects of particular admiration; tall, robust and beautifully formed, their faces beaming with delight and good humour, their teeth like ivory. They had distinct English features. The clothing of the young females consisted of a piece of linen reaching from the waist to the knees and a mantle thrown loosely over their shoulders. This covering seemed to be chiefly for protection from the sun as it was frequently set aside; it is was not possible to conceive more beautiful forms than they exhibited'.

On this same visit back to Weybourne, and the day before Esther's birthday, there is a tragic entry: '18th October. Awakened this morning with the dreadful news that one of Mr Ingham's vessels, the *Emily*, was ashore. Old Papa and William (WJJB) went down immediately and exerted themselves to the utmost. Only the Captain was saved. Hannah and I went down to the beach but we could only stand in the watch-house, the wind was so very high with frequent squalls'. The following day was calm and there was great activity, salvaging what could be recovered from the vessel between tides. The women were all down at the beach picking up coals.

The only evidence of WJJB and ship ownership concerns the *Enterprise*, a 126 ton schooner built at Morston, the next door creek to Blakeney, in 1842. The original Bill of Sale dated 22nd April 1846, now in the Norwich Record Office, shows that eleven owners 'transferred all their rights to William John Jennis Bolding of Weybourne, Gentleman and William Monement of Lynn Regis, Cork Manufacturer, both in the county of Norfolk and that in

William Monement (junior). c1855. He has a high starched collar with a stock and clearly was very clothes conscious and employed a high-class tailor.

the proportion of 30/64 shares to W.J.J.Bolding and 30/64 shares to William Monement bothaforesaid'. The remaining 4 shares were held by the widow of John Francis Johnson, WJJB's uncle. DerickMellor, studying the original log and account book of the *Enterprise* in the 1970s wrote the following: 'Between 1846 and 1853 the vessel traded as far afield as the Mediterranean bringing cork back to the Monement's cork factory in Lynn. With the cork it was necessary to have ballast. This was usually lead from Spain. The vessel came to Blakeney once each autumn to settle the account and pay over the profit to Bolding and Monement. The family went on board for a party if the weather was fine. One year there was little profit after payment had been made for two sailors left at Gibraltar because they were sick. They were collected on the next voyage, five months later; five month's lodging had to be paid for.' The original of the account book has disappeared, but fortunately a photocopy of it resides in the Norwich Record Office which I have looked at closely. A brief list of ports and cargoes makes interesting reading: April 1846 London ... May Newcastle COAL ... June Cadiz ... July Faro (Portugal) CORK ... Aug 23 Lynn ... 6 Oct Newcastle ... Dec 14 Cartagina (Spain) LEAD ... Jan 1847

ENDEAVOUR

Interpreting W.J.J.Bolding's October 1849 pencil drawing of the *Endeavour* raises more questions than it provides answers.

Through searching the King's Lynn shipping register, I have found that the vessel was built at Sutton in Yorkshire in 1826. It was almost certainly a Humber 'Billyboy', with one deck and one mast, sloop rigged with a topping up bowsprit. It was $54\frac{1}{2}$ft in length, $12\frac{3}{4}$ft in breadth and $5\frac{3}{4}$ft in depth, and tonnage was $40\frac{1}{2}$tons.

On 10th March 1847 it was registered at Wisbech. And on 1st February 1848 James Johnson was down as the owner. Further on in the docu-

The '*Endeavour, Lynn*' beached between Weybourne and Sheringham. A pencil drawing dated Oct.13th 1849 and signed WJJB

ment, the important statement was clearly written in two places: 'vessel foundered at sea 1849'.

The cargo of the *Endeavour* would presumably have been coal, to be loaded onto horse drawn carts on the beach at Weybourne. With the cliffs behind, the indications are that the vessel had beached a mile or two towards Sheringham, and not where intended. Was it driven ashore in stormy weather? Was it already unseaworthy, to be battered and broken up by the next gale, so prevalent at that time of the year, or did set sail again to return to King's Lynn and 'founder at sea'?

Faro (Portugal) CORK ... Mar 4 London ... Mar 23 Newcastle ... April 21 Shields COAL ... May 13 Exeter ... May 20 Brixham ... May 28 Newport IRON ... June 10 Hosley Bay ... June 20 Lynn ... June 26 Shields COAL ... July 14 Dartmouth ... July 25 Newport IRON ... Aug 8 Lynn. The vessel had a sad end, as recorded in the *Shipwreck Index* of R & B Larn: '*Enterprise* 04/01/1857 New Biggen-by-the-Sea voyage Newcastle to King's Lynn owner: Monement built 1842 Marston captain: Cornhill Drove ashore at 1 p.m. In wind conditions E force 10 accompanied by sleet, at low water, drifted off but struck again, and went to pieces'. No mention is made of the fate of the crew.

John Bolding died in 1847 and WJJB now inherited his father's estates throughout north Norfolk, built up through inheritance, marriage and purchase during previous decades. The family by now were without dispute the leading residents in Weybourne, and were to remain so until WJJB's death in 1899 and his nephew William Bolding Monement's death in 1925. Most of the family land in Weybourne was held copyhold from the Lord of the Manor. The meeting of the Manor Court on 7th December 1847 recorded that W.J.J.Bolding, on the death of his father John Bolding, was admitted to a total of 144 acres of land, houses and cottages, and the Ship Inn. A fine of £500 to the Lord of the Manor was to be paid. The detail in total ran to six full pages in the *Court Book*.

The family business interests were more than enough to keep WJJB at full stretch in his working years. Yet, here he was, particularly during the first decade after his father's death, away for parts of every year on painting trips, on archaeological field trips in Norfolk, and then there was his photography. Look closely at the splendid photograph of his mother, 'Old' Esther, taken in about 1855 (see over). She really does look a formidable lady, and surely must have been holding the reins during her son's frequent absences in the decade after her husband's death. And what about his sister Hannah? She may also have played an active role in the running of the business affairs.

In this first period after his father's death WJJB was active in acquiring property: in 1848 some land in Edgefield; and the same year land in Wey-

Esther Monement (1790-1868) (*née* Johnson of Cley), WJJB's mother. c1855.

bourne and also some copyhold through the Manor Court. In 1853 and 1855 he was buying again through the Manor Court. As always, the Census returns make interesting reading and, for the Boldings, give a clear indication of their fortunes at the time. In 1851 WJJB, aged 35, is down as Landed Proprietor farming 194 acres employing eleven, and as brewer employing three. His mother, 'Old' Esther, aged 60, is recorded as Land and House Proprietress. Living in the house were three female servants, aged twenty-six, nineteen and sixteen, and a thirty-one-year-old male groom and a nineteen-year-old 'employed in the brewery'. WJJB's sister Hannah was staying with Esther and family in King's Lynn. William Monement is down in the census as Cork Importer and Manufacturer, employing twelve hands. At this stage the Monements had three children: William Bolding Monement (born 1846), John Francis Bolding Monement (born 1849) and Mary Esther Monement (born January 1851).

When the Monement family came to Weybourne, which they seemed to do quite frequently, they stayed at 'The Cottage'. Hannah Beatrice Monement was born in December 1851, Martha Grace Monement in 1853, Eleanor Bolding Monement in 1854 and Cicely Anne Monement in 1856 (died 1858). As the family increased in size WJJB added on, again and again, to 'The Cottage', so that at his death at the end of the century there were eleven bedrooms and it could hardly be described as a cottage. Because of the way it had been put together, it was rambling and inconvenient in its layout.

I have in my possession WJJB's copy, in two volumes, of *Cyclopaedia of Useful Arts and Manufactures* edited by Charles Tomlinson and published in 1854 or thereabouts. Before the A-Z of subjects in the main part of the book there are CLX (160) pages of introduction, on the Great Exhibition of 1851. WJJB being the multi-talented person he was, will certainly have been to Hyde Park and one can imagine him making multiple visits; there was so much to see and Norwich to London by train had become possible in 1845. WJJB is unlikely to have clocked up the fifty visits made by the editor of the book! The exhibition was open from near the beginning of May until the 18th October in 1851 when there were over six million visits made. The editor calculated that if there were an average of two visits per person, that still meant that over three million people saw the exhibition. Tracking down the fledgling 'Photography' (invented for eleven years) in the 'Classification of the Objects Exhibited' was a lengthy process. "The objects are arranged into four principal groups and thirty classes: First, RAW MATERIALS, subdivided into four classes; secondly, MACHINERY, in six classes; thirdly, MANUFACTURES, in nineteen classes; and, fourthly, FINE ARTS". Where is 'Photography'? The answer is in MACHINERY – Class X 'Philosophical Instruments, and processes depending on their use.'.....Section D 'Application of Mechanical and Physical Science to Useful Purposes, not included in the preceding or subsequent sections.' .....3. LIGHT '- Instruments to assist vision: smaller Telescopes, Opera Glasses, Spectacles, Microscopes, Lenses, Mirrors, Lighthouses, Optical Illusions, Gas and Solar Microscopes, Cameras, Photography, Polarization of Light etc.' Well, I got there in the end. There were thousands of exhibits overall and the Great Exhibition, the brainchild of Prince Albert, was truly a wonder of the new Industrial Age.

It is relatively easy to identify the 'working' WJJB: the landowner, farmer, ship owner, maltster, brewer and multiple public house owner, but much more difficult is to pin down the threads of his 'hobbies' which played so large a part in his life, and his reputation as a remarkable man: artist, silhouettist, etcher, photographer; archaeologist, geologist, scientist; naturalist, botanist, gardener; taxidermist, jewellery maker, stone polisher and wood turner. One wonders how he managed.

An inspiration for WJJB's brilliant, inquiring mind will have lain with his first cousin once removed the genius Johnson Jex (c1778-1852). Jex's mother, a Johnson from Cley, married William Jex, the blacksmith of Billingford near Foulsham, in Cley church in 1773. Foulsham is fifteen miles or so inland from Cley and this is where Jex spent his early years and learnt his skills as a blacksmith. In 1802 Arthur Young, Secretary of the Board of Agriculture for England, published his volume *Agriculture in the County of Norfolk*. In the section on agricultural implements he wrote, 'I must not conclude without mentioning a person of extraordinary mechanical talent. He is a Mr Jex, a young blacksmith of Billingford.' There follows a description of various agricultural implements which Jex had invented or improved. Arthur Young also mentioned a machine which the young man had made for cutting watch pinnions, and goes on to say that 'Jex makes everything himself. He models and casts them in iron and brass, having a powerful wind furnace of his own invention'. Jex moved to Letheringsett, two miles inland from Cley, shortly after Young's glowing praise, where he took over as the village blacksmith from his grandfather. In addition to being a blacksmith and iron and brass founder, he also soon became a watchmaker, chronometer maker, glass blower, maker of thermometers, barometers and telescopes. He also made gear-cutting machines and lathes. (After his death his 'Triple Prismatic Engine Lathe' was 'purchased by W.J.J.Bolding, of Waborne').

Heating greenhouses with hot water pipes was newly invented and Jex applied himself to various mechanical inventions to develop this further. One was a self-regulating window for preserving a uniform degree of heat during the day in the greenhouse. This invention is explained by himself in a letter which he addressed to Thomas W.Coke, the Earl of Leicester, soliciting his patronage. The following is a short extract from the letter.

Letheringsett, August 18th, 1825
Sir,
Recently I have been engaged in perfecting an invention of my own relative to the forcing department of Horticulture, and I have now brought into successful action a self-regulating Light which I have applied to a small experimental Pine Pit; and it is adapted of course to Pine Stoves, Hot-houses, Green-houses, Conservatories etc.

Twenty-three days after Jex's death on 5th January 1852, W.H.Cozens-Hardy of Letheringsett Hall, gave a Lecture on the 'Life and Character of Johnson Jex, delivered in the British School Rooms, Holt'. In the Chair was H.R.Upcher of Sheringham Hall, near neighbour of WJJB. Without a doubt WJJB will have been at the lecture, the text of which was published in a booklet in 1855 after public demand.

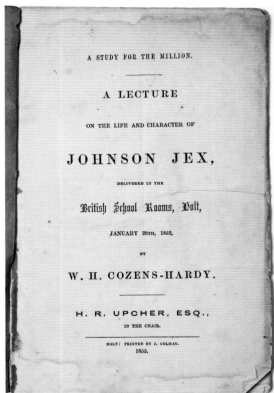

Title page of the lecture 'On the Life and Character of Johnson Jex, delivered in the British School Rooms, Holt 28th January 1852 by W.H.Cozens-Hardy – H.R.Upcher Esq., in the Chair – Holt: printed by J.Colman 1855'

'Entrance to Greenhouses'. The indications are that WJJB had several greenhouses.

It must be WJJB's copy that survives with me to this day. One paragraph in the lecture seems very pertinent. 'I find myself utterly incapable of doing justice to Jex as a man of science. It is probably that comparatively few of his successful experiments were ever made known to anyone, as he was always indisposed to reveal his inventions, even to his intimate friends, and undoubtedly many of his most important discoveries have perished with him'. In WJJB's large walled garden in Weybourne, in which there now stands an unattractive 20th-century house, is the ivy covered rusty metal frame of one of his greenhouses, sad looking but clearly defined. I have been informed that it had a very elaborate heating system. It is therefore quite clear that Johnson Jex's inspirational ideas on greenhouse heating were taken up by his equally versatile cousin. WJJB was thirty-six years old when Jex died; so for over twenty years would have had the opportunity to learn from the older man. How far, and in what others ways, did Jex's genius rub off on WJJB?

To refer to WJJB as a genius cannot be far off the mark as he was so able in so many areas of cultural life. It is his involvement with Norwich, the cultural centre of Norfolk, that is the key, but where is the evidence? A few snatches, here and there, but almost nothing. That he could hold his own with the elite in Norwich is beyond doubt having in mind his interest and expertise in so many areas.

Back in the 1970s when Derick Mellor was in the process of 'discovering' WJJB, he was directed towards Cliff Middleton, an expert on early photography, who identified the importance of WJJB's photographs. In the words of the editor of *Norfolk Fair* the two men 'tirelessly sifted through the letters and extant remains of his (WJJB's) work and

The ivy-covered metal struts of the remains of one of WJJB's greenhouses. c1995.

he has blossomed by their efforts from total obscurity to national importance'. As part of the King's Lynn Festival in 1977 there was a six week exhibition of WJJB's photographs, and some important pieces of family memorabilia, in the Museum of Social History. On 28th July Cliff Middleton gave a talk entitled 'W.J.J.Bolding – A Country Photographer'. A transcript of the talk was published in the September 1977 issue of *Norfolk Fair*. In it Middleton referred to Bolding being introduced to the 'Brotherhood, a cultural Norwich based society of educated men, who met to discuss arts, classics, science and anything of topical interest.' Middleton stated that the 'Brotherhood' learned of photography from Dr Hugh Welch Diamond, who recorded the faces of the insane in connection with his studies in medicine. Tremendous. But there is a problem. A few years ago I was informed that the 'Brotherhood' never existed; there never was an organisation under that name. What is quite clear is that WJJB did get in with a like-minded group of Norwich based educated men, where he would certainly have held his own, if not been centre stage.

When did this happen? Certainly by 1849 when WJJB started archaeological work with Henry Harrod, joint secretary of the newly-formed

HENRY HARROD (1817-71)

Harrod was born in Aylsham, Norfolk and educated in Norwich. He was admitted an attorney in Michaelmas term 1838, and was in practice for many years in Norwich. From the founding of the Norfolk and Norwich Archaeological Society in 1846 he was a joint secretary for the first twelve years, and contributed twenty papers to their *Transactions*. A few of these were as a result of his association with W.J.J.Bolding. During this period he collected the information which in 1857 he published in *Gleanings among the Castles and Convents of Norfolk*. In 1854 he became the secretary of the newly-founded Norfolk and Norwich Photographic Society, and in the same year he was named a fellow of the Society of Antiquities, for whose 'Proceedings' he wrote some articles, principally on matters concerning Norfolk.

In September 1857 at Hastings in Sussex, he married Mary, the daughter of Colonel Franklin Head, who was sixteen years his junior. They had two children: Henry and Frances. In 1862 the family moved to Marlborough in Wiltshire where Harrod entered into partnership with a solicitor, but three years later they moved to London, to Victoria Street, Westminster, where Harrod became a professional antiquary. He was remarkable for his skill in deciphering old documents, and was employed in arranging the records of Norwich, King's Lynn, and other boroughs. The New England Historic and Genealogical Society elected him a corresponding member. He was busy at work on a monograph on the Tower of London when he died at Clapham, Surrey on 24th January 1871.

Norfolk and Norwich Archaeological Society, and later the first secretary of the Norwich Photographic Society, and the two men will have become good friends. In the same year WJJB exhibited two oil paintings in the exhibition of the Norfolk and Norwich Society for the Promotion of the Fine Arts, when he must have met the brilliant young Norwich School artist John Middleton, if they had not already met before.

We have heard how WJJB may have been instructed by professional artists in his teenage years with his painting, and how he went away most years in May during the early years of his adulthood with his fishing gear and his sketching things, but it is not until 1848 that his surviving artistic output is regularly signed 'WJJB' and often dated. From these drawings one can see that in the majority of the years under discussion he made trips to many parts of Britain. Railway travel will have enthralled him, and he will certainly have made full use of this new form of transport which took him the length and breadth of our island; coaches maybe he took on occasions; hiring a pony and trap for local travel away from Norfolk seems his most likely means of transport.

In 1848 he made an extensive sketching trip to Wales. There are two brown monochrome drawings, heightened with white, of Vale Crucis Abbey in Denbighshire, one dated July 1848. In the valley nearby, the Pillar of Eliseg, dating from the 7th century and originally standing twelve feet high, warranted a pencil drawing; also a drawing of Llangollen, two miles away, which must have been from the same trip. Whether these were from the outward or return journey one can only speculate on. Much further west was a remote area about six miles from Snowdon at Bethgelert on the Carnarvonshire / Merionethshire borders where he drew an ancient bridge. A hundred-year-old gazetteer recorded: 'The village stands at the confluence of the Colwyn and Glaslyn rivers near Aberglaslyn Pass. It nestles in a deep romantic vale, engirt by lofty mountains, amidst the grandest scenery in Wales; presents very strong attractions to tourists, artists and anglers.' In fact ideal territory for WJJB. Not far away lies the pass of Aberglaslyn, which also drew WJJB's attention. 'It is one of the grandest and most romantic passes in Wales. It is a deep gorge, the cliffs, almost perpendicular on one side, approaching so closely as to barely leave room for the road and river. Through it flows the Glaslyn, a mountain torrent, whirling its clear waters over its boulder-stream bed, and forming a fall at the extremity of the pass, where an ivy-clad stone bridge of one arch, called Pont Aberglaslyn, stretches from rock to rock.' Further south in Merionethshire a drawing of Bala Lake and several of Harlech Castle may have been from this trip, but he was certainly at Harlech in 1857. 1850 was the year that WJJB was sketching in Switzerland. Thank goodness that two of the brown monochrome drawings are dated. A drawing done in Antwerp and another in

Harlech Castle with Snowdon in the distance. Either from a WJJB sketching trip in 1848 or from one in the 1850s

Rouen indicate the likely route to the Swiss Alps and back. His touring in Switzerland was extensive, so it must have been quite a long visit. Not surprisingly, in view of his interest in archaeology, he visited the ruins of

Left: 'WJJB 1850 Switzerland Grindelwald' Brown wash drawing.

Above: Chateau de Chillon on the shore of Lake Geneva. Brown wash drawing with white highlight 1850.

'Land's End' grey wash drawing with white highlight. c1850.

Aventicum, the capital of Roman Switzerland, beside the modern town of Avenches. Not far from there is Lake Murten (Morat to WJJB) and there is a lovely brown monochrome wash drawing of the town from the lake. Nearly one hundred miles to the east, right in the centre of Switzerland, Mount Pilatus near Lucerne took his attention. Fifty or so miles to the south, near the Italian border, are Realp and the remote Furka Pass, 2436 metres, almost 8000 feet, above sea level. Then west about fifty miles to intimidating views at Lauterbrunnen and Grindelwald. Finally, west another one hundred miles to Lake Leman and two brown monochrome drawings of the Castle of Chillon, one a stunning example heightened in white. There does not seem to be any evidence of another overseas sketching trip.

Castles and monastery sites were always a great pull for WJJB and two drawings in Cumberland in 1853 support his interest: to Naworth Castle not far from Brampton and Roman Emperor Hadrian's Wall, and Lanercost Priory in the same parish. 1854 saw him the eastern side of the Pennines in Northumberland at Hexham and Corbridge. The next year a dated drawing from Teignmouth in Devon pinpoints his going down to the far west. The fine undated drawings at Land's End must emanate from this trip. He was back to Wales in 1857, ten years on from his last visit. Whether on his way there or the way back he drew the mill at Guy's Cliff in Warwickshire. Again he was up near Snowdon; then Portmadoc and Tremadoc, and on for a return visit to Harlech Castle.

'Ben Nevis' signed WJJB. c1850.

A handful of drawings record a sketching trip to Scotland, the date of which is unknown. Did he go north of the border with his brilliant young friend John Middleton? A most evocative grey wash drawing high up on Ben Nevis has an eagle hovering; on a ledge below, the carcass of a sheep straddles a rock.

The twenty or so silhouettes by WJJB that survive help to show his amazing all round talent and desire to experiment in all artistic fields. Only one of his silhouette subjects can be named, and that was of his much younger first cousin Hannah Johnson from Salthouse who was born in 1840. By the looks of her age WJJB drew her between 1846 and 1848. This would be just before his involvement in the world of photography. The name 'silhouette' comes from Etienne de Silhouette (1709-67), a French minister of finance, who did not invent the process, but was fascinated by the 'black shade' process as it was known then, and is said to have plastered rooms in his chateau with cut-out portraits. Silhouettes were considered as the 'poor man's miniature' and were hugely popular until the invention of photography (see page 59).

It is clear that WJJB was introduced to the new art of photography by his friends from the Norwich artistic and intellectual group. There is no evidence that WJJB took photographs before Frederick Scott Archer had introduced his wet collodion glass plate negative technique in 1851 which produced albumen prints. It was the most frequently used negative process up until the mid-1880s and the one that WJJB followed. It will have taken time before this new idea came to Norwich, so it is unlikely, from the evidence, that WJJB took his first photographs before 1852 or early 1853.

In 1854 the Norfolk Photographic Society was founded, with WJJB's friend Henry Harrod as secretary. Thomas Lound, William Freeman and John Middleton, all Norwich School artists of the younger generation, were committee members. The first exhibition of the Norwich Photographic Society took place in November 1856 at the Exhibition Rooms, Broad Street, Norwich. The catalogue identifies the photographs taken by WJJB:

West door, Castle Acre priory. c1855 (Norfolk County Council).

No.	Subject	Negative
81	North Runcton church chancel	wax
202	Gateway, Castle Rising	wax
340	South-west tower, Castle Acre priory	wax
341	West door, Castle Acre priory	wax
157	Portraits	coll.
195	Portraits	coll.

('wax' means waxed-paper negative and 'coll.' means collodion negative)

The *Norfolk News* for 3rd January 1857 was unequivocal in its praise, describing WJJB's photographic images as 'perhaps the finest proofs we have seen from waxed paper, on account of the unusual transparency of the shadows'.

Also there were the two exhibits from that exhibition entitled 'Portraits'. These were photographs of village people and WJJB's employees in Weybourne, images, along with photographs of family members and friends, on which his photographic reputation is largely based. Early photographers did not tend to photograph ordinary working people in their everyday working clothes, but this is what WJJB did. He seems to have

South-west tower, Castle Acre priory, Norfolk. c1855.

Unknown men. c1855.

1 A scene in the farmyard behind 'The House', with good examples of farm wagons and a hay drying rack behind. Front left is a heap of mangolds, cattle feed in the winter. The real interest in this photograph is the large window on the building on the left. This was the north window of WJJB's photographic studio on the first floor of the barn. There was one window on the east wall, one on the south and two on the west. Morning photography took place at the northern end of the studio, and in the afternoon down at the southern end.

2 A modern view of WJJB's studio, c1995, showing the south and east windows.

3 The farmyard behind 'The House', with hay drying racks and a shepherd's hut for the lambing season. c1855.

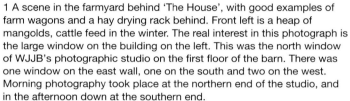

deliberately set out to capture the dress and trades of the people who worked for him, and most of the sitters hold or wear some clue to their occupation. It is remarkable that ordinary working people from a hundred and fifty years ago should be remembered in photographs when the most they could expect would be a record in a church burial register, and a headstone in a churchyard, if they were lucky.

WJJB's Weybourne home, The House, is now the Maltings hotel. Across the yard and only yards from the hotel itself is a barn, the down-

Left and jacket: This is probably WJJB's earliest surviving photograph - late 1853/early 1854. William and Esther Monement are with their four eldest children: William Bolding and John Francis Bolding, and the two girls born in 1851, Mary Esther and Hannah Beatrice.

Right: William Monement with his two boys and one of the girls. c1854.

stairs of which was converted into an outside bar for the hotel, in use until a few years ago. The window distribution of the first floor level shows clearly that this area, as one large room, was WJJB's photographic studio. Facing north is an outsize window, with large windows on the east and west walls. It is obvious that morning photography took place up this end of the upstairs room. The upstairs south wall window is also large and there is an outsize window on the west wall. At this end, in the middle of the day and in the afternoon, willing, and maybe not so willing, sitters were ushered, week after week and year after year to have their images taken. We, in the 21st century, are the beneficiaries of all those portrait sessions.

A plain linen or canvas backcloth was hung on the wall of the studio, and on the floor a mottled carpet sometimes covered the wooden planks, other times a piece of linen, and others the bare boards themselves. Many of the village working people and tradespeople, almost all of whom are seated, are holding their props. The same chairs appear again and again, but often are hidden by the large size of the men or the wide flowing dresses of the women. One chair is a slender mahogany chair with arms

St Margaret's Church, King's Lynn from the High Street. c1855.

dating from the Regency period, and another a high upright chair without arms, much older. A small square-topped tripod table was often used when photographing the family and visiting friends, with books and framed photographs as props. It has often been stated that early photographic portraits have a 'wooden' feeling, the sitters looking awkward and ill at ease. It is to WJJB's great credit, and his great skill, that most of his sitters look relaxed and at ease.

One of the earliest of WJJB's photographs identified is of his sister Esther, with her husband William, and their four eldest children: William Bolding Monement (b.1846), John Francis Bolding Monement (b.1849), Mary Esther (Marietta) Monement (b.January 1851) and Hannah Beatrice Monement (b.December 1851). The two girls look to be no more than two years old which puts the date at the end of 1853 or the first half of 1854. Only the parents are anywhere near in focus, the children not being able to sit still for long enough. I have studied many family photographs of WJJB's nephews and nieces, and the dating is done by posing the question as to the age of the sitter or sitters. From that an approximate date is given – not scientific, but a rough guide. Identification of the nephews and nieces is helped in that first there are the two boys, then the two girls born in the same year; then two more girls, Martha Grace Monement (b.1853) and Eleanor Bolding Monement (b.1854). Francis William (Frank) Monement (b.1858) followed next, but either side of him were a sister and brother who died very young. Finally two more girls: Rose Cecily Monement (b.1860) and Maude Marguerite Monement (b.1861). Frank was so much younger than the other boys, and the six girls fitted neatly into pairs, with the first four being so much older than the last two, that the identification process is made somewhat easier.

It is unlikely that WJJB took many photographs away from his own village. Apart

Looking down Crown and Anchor Street, Weybourne with the maltings building on the left and the church tower beyond. c1855.

from the images of buildings in the 1856 Norwich exhibition only one photograph of St Margaret's Church in King's Lynn (only very recently being promoted to Minster status), one of Swaffham church from the market place, and one of an unidentified ruined castle keep are known. A number of farm buildings and street scenes in Weybourne were recorded over the years, and views in WJJB's garden, including the greenhouse, but it is WJJB's portraits that make the greatest impression.

Child discipline in the mid 19th century was very different to that of the modern time, which I know only too well when thinking of my grandchildren. It is remarkable that WJJB's nephews and nieces were able to remain absolutely still for the necessary time of the long exposure at such a young age. Many of the group portraits involving two or more of his nephews and nieces show that he must have spent considerable time in preparing them for the photograph, a procedure that would have taxed their patience and concentration; the results on some are so spectacular for their naturalness that one marvels at WJJB's creative ability, and his ability to keep his young sitters 'on side'.

The evidence for WJJB's art, archaeology and photography is much easier to identify during the ten years after his father's death in 1847 than in any other period of his life. In 1857 he was forty-two, exactly half way through the eighty-four years when he died. The evidence for his art comes almost to a standstill. Drawings dated 1858 of Sandown Bay and Bonchurch St Clair tell us that he was on the Isle of Wight, and the following year a drawing of Teignmouth shows that he was back in Devon. The only other dated art is a brown wash drawing of 1861 signed 'Badger Valley, Waborne'. Was John Middleton's death in 1856 a strong factor in what could be described as rapid decline of interest in that field?

Evidence for archaeology seemed now to be centred around Weybourne priory ruins and church, which remained a stronghold until old age and poor health drew a close. Family photographs, in considerable numbers, survive right through the decades and indicate no lessening of interest, though in his later years they are of individuals or groups photographed for the record rather than with any planned artistic intent, as in earlier times.

'In Badger Valley June 11th 1861 WJJB'.
Brown wash drawing.

The market place, Swaffham looking towards the church. c1855.

A surveyor/architect. A number of farm buildings in Weybourne have the initials 'WJJB' and date on a gable end.

John Digby. c1855. He is recorded as the drayman who delivered barrels of beer to Aylsham and collected the cash payments for them.

Through the years WJJB continued to increase his land holdings in Weybourne and elsewhere when the opportunity arose. In 1861 he purchased two cottages through the Manor Court for £115, and in 1872, also through the Manor Court, five cottages, a yard and garden. In June 1877, again through the Court, from William Bird of Hempstead and David Dady of Waborne one hundred and twenty-six acres of land. The sum paid was £1999. 0. 0, with the fine to the Lord of the Manor of £237. 0. 0. Serious money. September 1877 saw another purchase through the Manor Court. Away from Weybourne, at an auction at the Feathers Inn, Holt on 30th June 1876 just over seven acres of land in Cley, adjoining his family land, was bought for £590. Over £80 an acre seems a very high price. On the Memorandum of Agreement WJJB's signature is below the statement, 'I acknowledge that the above lot was purchased by me as agent for and on behalf of Miss Hannah Elizabeth Bolding.' In 1952, by compulsory purchase of the Erpingham Rural District Council for the building of 'Houses for the Working Classes', about half of that land was sold for £100 an acre.

The Norwich Record Office houses an insignificant little red cash book which is itemised as 'W.F.Hill (Wine Merchant) of Aylsham in account with W.J.J.Bolding Esq.' The years covered are 1856 to 1861. Hill was buying beer from WJJB's Weybourne Brewery – Beer £1.15. 0d a barrel; Stout £2.13. 0d a barrel; Ale £2.13. 0d a barrel; Porter {a dark-brown malt liquor, i.e. a brown beer, probably so called because of being a favourite drink of porters in London} £2.13. 0d a barrel. Almost all entries say 'cash by John Digby' – WJJB's man delivering the beer to Aylsham. The best year was 1860 when Hill's purchases came to just over £220 for the year, with at least one purchase every month.

A document traced through Google stated that WJJB owned Fakenham Tower Mill in 1861 having paid £180, and that he sold it to James Stone of Fakenham on 5th July 1882 for £70. Clearly not a successful business venture. I have been left wondering how many more pieces of evidence relating to WJJB's business life are lurking in dark corners. Only very recently deeds, in his name, relating to the Calthorpe Arms public house in Blakeney, which he sold to the Norwich brewers Steward and Patteson in 1897, appeared at a local history display in the village. What more sur-

Frank Monement showing off (as he was wont) with his banjo. Did you notice it lying on the piano in the drawing room at 'The House'? c1880.

prises are there in store?

A few years back I saw a large account book of a shop in Holt where WJJB's name appeared only once, in 1881. The shop seemed to sell almost everything. WJJB's purchases were: Rangoon Oil 1/-, Glycerine & Ag Rose 1/, Aqua Potash 2/6, honey soap 1/6, Powalls Balsam 2/3, Blue Dye 6d and carbolic acid 1/-; an interesting and varied selection.

The only mention of WJJB's connection with geology, apart from his link with John Middleton, was his nephew William Bolding Monement's 1925 obituary when it was stated that 'his uncle as a scientist might have well ranked with the great ones of the day. When the British Association (for the Advancement of Science) last came to Norwich (in 1868), the geologists were satisfied to accept Mr Bolding's papers on the Norfolk Drift'.

In 1871 WJJB found himself as Director of

WJJB oil painting of Weybourne and the priory church. It is hanging on the far wall in the drawing room.

Hannah Bolding in the garden 1880s.

The interior of Weybourne church. c1870 with the old box pews, before the north aisle was added in the 1880s.

Fieldwork on the Norfolk and Norwich Archaeological Society survey of Weybourne priory and church. No better man for the task in hand. WJJB's interest over the years had clearly been concerned with the archaeology of the site and not with the interior of the parish church. Volume X of *Norfolk Archaeology* (1888) on 'The Augustinian priory at Weybourne, Norfolk – communicated by Rev. C.R.Manning F.S.A., Hon. Sec. Read at Weybourne Sept. 21st 1883' had a number of mentions of WJJB: 'For many years past Mr Bolding has been a careful investigator of the original plan of these ruins (Weybourne priory), and has laid down what he considers to have been the disposition of the buildings at several different periods of their history.' Later in the same article, 'After seeing the masonry that remains in the west wall of the tower on the south side, with evident traces of the springing of the circular arch, and after a study of the valuable plans which Mr Bolding has from time to time put on record, as he investigated the foundations to the west of the tower, I feel convinced that Mr Freeman was in error supposing that the tower was a western one, and not central.' (Prof. E.A.Freeman (1823-92) was an eminent Victorian historian and was a prolific writer, often concerning the medieval period. It was a reference in his book *English Towns and Districts* that Rev. Manning took issue with). The 1925 obituary of William Bolding Monement, with a reference to his uncle WJJB, put the case slightly differently: 'The plan of Weybourne church – its original ground plan which has been altered during centuries – remained with Professor Freeman as a puzzle until he saw Mr Bolding's plan, which he accepted at once.'

The welfare of the parish church of All Saints, Weybourne, featured strongly in the lives of the Bolding family, many of whom are buried in the churchyard outside the tower to the west. Until the restoration towards the end of the 19th century, the church consisted of the chancel, nave tower and porch. A worshipper would have sat in small square box pews, surrounded by plain walls, only relieved by the announcement in large letters over the chancel arch that 'this church was new pew'd Anno Domini 1817. John Bolding, Churchwarden' (WJJB's father). A photograph of the inside of the church, taken by WJJB in about 1870, to a certain extent supports the view of Dr Jessop (whose essay on the Episcopal visitations of

Left: WJJB in his garden in the 1880s, photographed by his niece Rose Monement.

Right: WJJB and his sister Hannah photographed on the steps of the entrance porch to 'The House' by their niece Rose Monement late 1880s.

monastic houses in the diocese of Norwich was published in the 1880s), who spoke about Weybourne church as being 'a poverty-stricken build-ing'. In 1888 the church was completely restored and new roofed in oak. The former chancel of the original Saxon church was rebuilt and added to the church as a north aisle. The total cost came to £1044, most likely paid for, in large part, by WJJB and the Earl of Orford, the Lord of the Manor.

The document in the Norfolk Record Office showing four different coloured plans of Weybourne priory puts the importance of WJJB's role quite clearly. It is signed: 'W.J.J.Bolding, Waborne – 1830 to 1891'. Sixty-one years, from the ages of fifteen to seventy-six. It seems to be making the point that here, with the onset of old age and failing health, a chapter of his life is being laid to rest.

In 1892 WJJB's sister Hannah, with whom he had lived all their lives, died age seventy-six. The old man was to live for another seven years, with his two nephews and four unmarried nieces close at hand. Almost no events are recorded, but photographs survive of a dramatic rescue

THE WRECK OF THE *IDA*

Photographs 1, 2 and 4 were taken by either WJJB or his niece Rose. Would the seventy-seven year old WJJB venture out on a blustery February day to walk two or three miles along the beach, a task the thirty-three-year-old Rose would take in her stride? According to the information in R. and B. Larn's *Shipwrecks on the East Coast* the *Ida* was 345 tons and had a crew of ten. There are seventeen men in the photograph taken against the stern of the ves-sel, so seven are locals. It was recorded that after being fed by people from the village the crew helped to salvage some of the timbers, including the bowsprit, which survive in cottages and barns in the village. The photograph of the rocket and line is shown. Many many seamen's lives were now saved, when in the past it was more than likely that they would have drowned in the surf on the gale-swept beaches.

1 The ten man crew of the *Ida*, with some of their rescuers photographed against the stern of the vessel.

2 The *Ida* a few days after coming ashore.

3 An example of the life-saving rocket and line (not from the family collection, but produced by Derick Mellor in the 1970s).

4 The *Ida* six months later.

Eastern Daily Press Thursday 23rd February 1893

WRECK OF A BARQUE OFF SHERINGHAM – GALLANT RESCUES

The Norwegian barque *Ida*, bound from Christiansand to Cardiff, is ashore between Lower Sheringham and Weybourne, at a little west of where the steam trawler Magneta stranded a few months ago. The vessel, of which a Norwegian named Tonnesen is captain, struck about half past four yesterday morning. Signals of distress were soon seen from both Sheringham and Weybourne and efforts were at once put on foot for saving the crew. Great fears were entertained, but after several unsuccessful attempts by both the Sheringham and Weybourne life saving companies, the former succeeded in getting a rocket line into the rigging of the vessel. It was then found that the line had become entangled. However the next shot by the Weybourne company reached its intended goal. Then followed a grand exhibition of life saving. The first to land was a boy, the men standing on the beach to haul him ashore. It was however found necessary to take the hawser to the top of the cliff, and the rest of the crew were safely landed. Lusty cheers were sent up when the last man, the captain, reached the shore about 8 o'clock. Scarcely had he reached terra firma when two of the masts of the barque went over the side. Against one of those the captain had been standing. The Dudgeon light, it is believed, was mistaken for the North End light, and it being a rough and dirty night, this accounts for the stranding of the barque. It is expected she will become a total wreck. She is 329 tons register and laden with pit props. The vessel is now breaking up.

Eastern Daily Press Monday 27th February 1893

SHERINGHAM – THE WRECK

The barque that stranded on Wednesday morning has become a complete wreck. The cargo, being so very far from town, is of very little worth. A party of Lynn men are working at the wreck, the Sheringham men being unable to come to satisfactory terms. It is expected that the cargo – pit props – will be laid on the beach, and disposed of by public auction.

from a three-hundred-ton Norwegian barque, the *Ida*, which came ashore on the beach near Weybourne on 22nd February 1893. Whether the photographs were taken by WJJB or his niece Rose one cannot be sure. The rescue was made by rocket and line and all the crew were saved.

In 1895 WJJB entered his ninth decade, almost certainly in poor health. It was about time to think about putting his affairs in order. In 1897 he must have closed the Weybourne Brewery because in that year he sold fourteen public houses in north Norfolk to the Norwich brewers Steward and Patteson. (The Angel, Holt; the Blue Bell, Wiveton; The Bull. Thurgarton; The Calthorpe Arms, Blakeney; The Crown and Anchor, Weybourne; The George and Dragon, Cley; The Fishing Boat, East Runton; The Lobster, Sheringham; The King's Head, Cromer; The Ship, Weybourne; The White Horse, Edgefield; The White Horse, Overstrand; The Unicorn, Aylsham).

It must have been in the early years of the 20th century that the main maltings building, right on the village street in front of 'The House', was demolished. Now there is no reminder, except in the name of what was WJJB's home all his life: 'The Maltings Hotel'.

In January 1898 WJJB wrote his will (see Apendix III page 167). He lived for nearly two more years, witnessing two more springs, two more summers and autumns, but only one more winter. In 1899 he died on Trafalgar Day, 21st October. He was the leading resident in Weybourne and there will have been a large turnout for his funeral: family, friends, people from the village, former employees on his farmland and in the brewery. Also those who had benefited from his 'kindly nature and unostentatious charity' which 'had won for him universal respect and esteem'. How many of those present had been photographed by the deceased decades before? Fifteen months after WJJB died so did his queen. The Victorian age was over and it was the end of an era.

The grave of WJJB and his sister Hannah Bolding in the ruins of Weybourne priory church.

The First Eleven

W.J.J. Bolding's top photographs as selected by John Benjafield

The Man with a Cloak. This magnificent profile was photographed probably in the mid-1850s. A visitor to Weybourne or an estate worker, we shall never know. With a cloak tightly held over his right shoulder the sitter projects 'noble strength' and demonstrates WJJB's mastery of the close-up in a way not surpassed by any of his other portraits (Norfolk County Council).

The Boy with a Lathe. WJJB's nephew, William Bolding Monement is seen here operating a wood lathe. Following the publication of a woodturning reference book published by Holtzapffel in 1850, woodturning became the principal hobby of the mechanically-minded English gentry who produced a wide range of complex ornamental turnings. It's not, therefore, surprising that William is seen here doing just that. c1856.

The Boy with a Knife. Robert Digby, 'Silent Robert', wearing a cotton jacket, corduroy trousers and peaked cap, projects a menacing image as he looks intently off left while holding his knife as if ready to be put into use. This is an extraordinary, masterly photograph made in the 1850s.

89

The Fine Close-Up. William Monement wearing a stylish, wide-brimmed straw hat and a wide bow tie on an upturned collar. The lighting is perfect to capture this fine close-up portrait which fills the photograph. c1855.

The Woodland Path. WJJB again demonstrates his mastery of the camera with this image of the leafy pathway through the woods, said to be Badger Valley, Weybourne. His depth of field shows sunlight reflected off tree trunks, leaves and ferns both near and far; we are transported back in time, over more than 150 years.

The Family Triangle. Arranged in a pleasing triangular format, it is not immediately clear that in this family group one girl is lying on the rug with her head resting on her brother's knee. In her arms, Esther Monement is holding Eleanor Bolding and Hannah, Beatrice, John, Francis Bolding and Mary Esther are seated (left to right) on the rug with Martha Grace lying down. It seems WJJB was very persuasive with children as only two of them are looking at the camera during exposure. The carefully placed pompom dahlias, basket of apples and cut barley show it's harvest time. Not only is the loving family portrayed but its wealth is clearly on display. c1860.

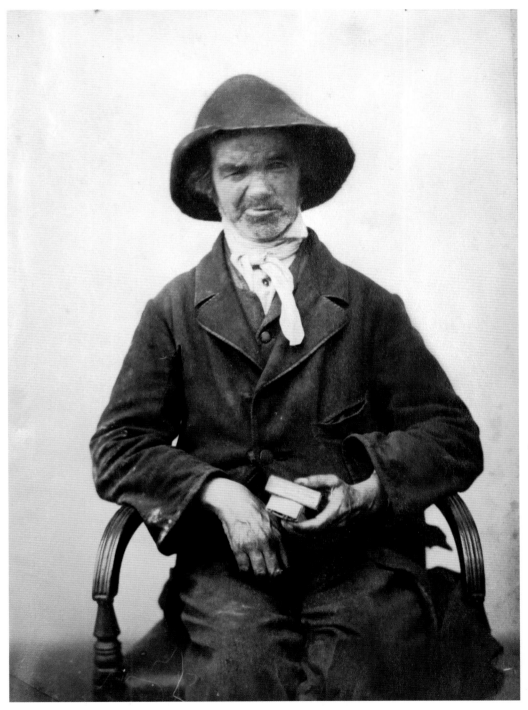

The Smoker. This slender villager, wearing a tough but worn overcoat and a soft felt hat seems quite relaxed as he looks at the camera. One of the two boxes clasped in his left hand is a matchbox and another photograph shows him smoking a clay pipe. c1855.

Children with a Doll. Hannah Beatrice Monement, seated, looks lovingly at her doll which she holds just as her mother would hold her baby, and her sister Mary Esther, half-smiling and looking away from the camera, holds a hat while gently leaning against the chair. The angular structure of this composition draws our eyes across the image. c1860.

The Brewer. In pensive mood, WJJB's brewer, Bill Digby, protects his clothing with a hessian sack roped around his waist. His necktie has a small bow and his sleeves are rolled up internally. He's holding a derby hat, made of hard felt with a flat top, which had been specially designed in 1850 for the servants of William Coke, 2nd Earl of Leicester, of Holkham Hall. Perhaps the necktie and hat set the brewer apart from his labourers. c1855.

The First Gun. William Bolding Monement, aged about 14, seen here wearing a jacket, waistcoat and bow tie, holds a shotgun, the stock between his legs and the barrel resting inside his elbow. The sons of wealthy rural parents were often taught to shoot for sport. c1860.

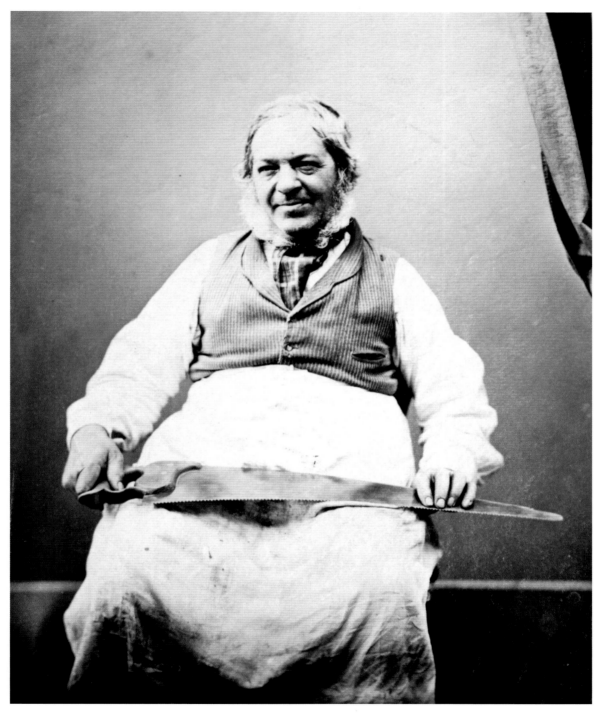

The Furniture Maker. Shown here wearing his apron, the smiling furniture maker, Sam Dady, is gently tensing his handsaw across his knees. He seems very relaxed in the presence of his employer. The curling edge of the backdrop adds to the image. c1855.

Chapter 5

WJJ Bolding and John Middleton

One friendship of WJJB's that is well documented was with the brilliant later Norwich School artist John Middleton, who tragically died of consumption at the early age of twenty-nine. Middleton was born in Norwich into a well-to-do family in 1827, and his father owned a painting and decorating business in the city. His mother died in 1830 when he was a toddler. (His father remarried, so the Mrs Middleton referred to later was his stepmother.) Little is known of his early life, but he certainly became a pupil of John Berney Ladbrooke (1803-79), whose work placed emphasis on rural landscapes and especially to studies of trees. Ladbrooke had been a pupil of John Crome (1768-1821), his uncle, the founder, along with his father Robert Ladbrooke (1769-1842) of the Norwich Society of Artists, and famous for his woodland scenes. There was thus a strong link between the founders of the Norwich School of Artists and Middleton. Later Middleton received instruction from Henry Bright (1810-73), whose watercolour style was clearly seen in his pupil's work. With Middleton's watercolours and in his etchings, barns, trees, felled timber, fences, gates and water dominate his compositions. By 1847 at the age of twenty he reached the peak of his artistic talent, and a selection of his watercolours from that year held in Norwich Castle are proof of his brilliance. In that same year he went to London, but his time there was cut short when his

John Middleton pencil drawing in the family collection. c1852.

Top: John Middleton scraperboard of the ford of the river Glaven at Glandford. c1852.

Bottom: WJJB oil painting 'The Ford of the Glaven' exhibited in Norwich in 1853.

99

John Middleton scraperboard of a Norfolk river scene. c1852.

'Drawn expressly for Miss Bolding! (Hannah Bolding WJJB's unmarried sister) by John Middleton'. On the back of the river scene scraperboard.

father died the following year, and he returned to Norwich to the family business, and resided in the city for the rest of his short life.

Middleton made a number of sketching trips to far flung corners of Britain: to the Isle of Arran, Scotland (1847 and 1853), Wales (1847 and 1855) and Devon (1850 and 1851), while, nearer to Norfolk, he was in Kent on an extensive sketching trip with Henry Bright in 1848, at Hatfield, Hertfordshire in the same year, and at Henley and other places on the river Thames, possibly in 1851. Did WJJB accompany Middleton on any of these long distance trips? We know that WJJB sketched in Scotland as far north as Ben Nevis, also in North Wales and at Land's End in Cornwall. That the two men travelled together out of Norfolk is not in doubt. Three letters from Middleton to WJJB survive and one dated March 1854 letter stated, 'I shall be very glad to go to Lynn with you – but hope that will not interfere with our Suffolk excursion.'

Between 1847 and 1855 Middleton exhibited in London at the Royal Academy and the British Institution, as well as in Norfolk at the Norfolk and Norwich Association for the Promotion of the Fine Arts, and he achieved contemporary recognition in both cities. He was also a skilful etcher and in 1852 published a book of nine etchings which show through his subtlety of line that he was a deserving heir to John Crome in the medium of etching. He was a keen photographer in the early days of photography in Norfolk. The only images attributed to him are a group of views in North Wales (held in the Norwich Castle Museum and Art Gallery) which show the quality of his artistic vision.

WJJB and Middleton may well have first met in 1849, when WJJB, as an Associate of the Norfolk and Norwich Association for the Promotion of the Fine Arts, exhibited two oil paintings: 'Near Weybourne' (catalogue no. 111) and 'Weybourne' (catalogue no. 220). They may well have met earlier, but what is not in doubt is that they became good friends, and Middleton stayed with the Bolding family in Weybourne on an unknown number of occasions up to his last illness. A meaningful percentage of Middleton's artistic output in the last years of his life were executed around Weybourne or the nearby north Norfolk area, a clear indication of his staying at Weybourne and going on sketching trips from there, and sometimes certainly with WJJB. The March 1854 letter had Middleton writing, 'A visit of a few days at Weybourne will be very gratifying to me and I shall hope to avail myself of your kind invitation in April.'

WJJB oil painting of a harvest scene on the field behind 'The House'. c1845. His postmill, the watermill house, and the coastguard cottages on the beach at Weybourne can be easily recognised.

Examples of the two men's output complement each other directly, notably Middleton's scraper board of the ford of the river Glaven at Glandford and WJJB's most accomplished oil, exhibited in Norwich in 1853 ('The Ford of the Glaven' Catalogue no. 38). This was the first place up the tidal estuary where, in ancient times, it was possible to ford the river Glaven with any certainty. The two men were on the same bank of the river only a short distance apart when sketching. On the far bank, on higher ground, in both men's pictures stands the ruin of Glandford church, its tower standing proud, but the nave and chancel open to the elements and in full decay. At the end of the 19th century Sir Alfred Jodrell (1847-1929), the owner of Bayfield Hall and all that constituted the hamlet of Glandford, was to build a model village there, a museum for his huge collection of shells, and, in memory of his mother, to completely rebuild the church. Today the ford, with a modern

Photograph. c1855 from the farmyard looking north, showing many of the features seen in the oil, but with clothes drying on the hedge.

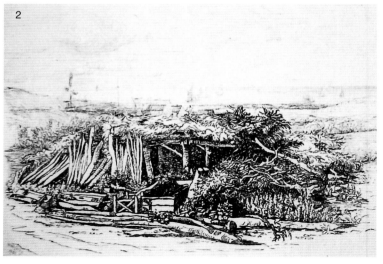

1 John Middleton etching. c1852.

2 WJJB etching. c1852.

3 John Middleton's etching reversed. The mill and the hay drying rack show exactly where Middleton was sitting for this etching.

4 WJJB's etching reversed. A heavy example – probably WJJB's first etching attempt.

pedestrian bridge, is still a place of great atmosphere, where small children feed the ducks and swans, and the occasional tractor and high rise four wheel drive vehicle cross from one bank to another, a short cut saving several miles (see page 99).

Apart from Middleton's scraper board of Glandford, two more are in the possession of family descendants. One depicts a windmill in a landscape scene, maybe the same mill above Sheringham (now Upper Sheringham) in a watercolour by Henry Bright. The other, of a river bank scene, with the ever popular Middleton gate and fence, is very special because, on the back, in pencil, is written, 'Drawn expressly for Miss Bolding! by John Middleton'. Miss Bolding was WJJB's unmarried sister Hannah who shared 'The House' with him and their mother, 'Old' Esther.

Most of Middleton's etchings were drawn as he saw them, so were printed in reverse. A tiny example (60x40mm) only comes clear when it is reversed, and all is revealed. The artist was sitting in the farmyard behind 'The House' in Weybourne, looking north with the North Sea in the distance. Compare this with a WJJB oil painting and photograph from a very similar position. The sequence is completed with a WJJB etching, probably his first effort using the technique which is full of heavy detail; when it is reversed, it shows that it was etched from approximately the same position as Middleton's etching. (A copy of WJJB's etching is in the Fitzwilliam Museum in Cambridge.)That WJJB was introduced to the etching process by Middleton is a logical assumption, and encouraged and coached by him too. WJJB's only other known etching, of the Easter Sepulchre in Kelling church (near Holt), is finely drawn, and of remarkable quality.

The Easter sepulchre, Kelling church
WJJB etching. c1854.

A collection of WJJB photographs of trees, and trees with water, automatically have me thinking of Middleton. Ever since I saw the photographs nearly thirty years ago I had the image in my mind that Middleton took copies of the photographs back to Norwich and pinned them on the wall of his studio and used them to help him plan his drawings. One particular photograph has all the ingredients of a typical Middleton watercolour or etching. There are trees, a fence, a gate and water. It has everything.

In December 2010 I bid for and purchased, at a Bonham's Auction in Bury St Edmunds, a Middleton pencil drawing heightened with white body colour, of Sheringham Hall, only two miles from WJJB's home, signed JM and dated 1852. I was desperate to buy it. Pencil, with white

A fine specimen of a tree. c1855.

highlight, was a favourite technique of WJJB's. Two drawings by him of Sheringham Park in that medium, dated September 1849, are in my collection. Middleton will no doubt have looked through the range of WJJB's artistic output, and I'm sure the older man will have sought comment and advice from his much more talented friend. Pencil and wash heightened with white was an unusual medium for Middleton. Henry Bright used extensive white highlighting, but I like to believe Middleton's Sheringham Hall drawing was executed because he had seen WJJB's work, from 1849, and was encouraged by it to produce his own in the same medium (see page 106).

It is clear that WJJB and Middleton shared a number of interests other than art, and this is confirmed in the Middleton letters to WJJB. In 1854 the Norfolk Photographic Society was founded, with WJJB's friend Henry Harrod as secretary. Thomas Lound, William Freeman, Norwich School artists of the younger generation, and Middleton, were committee members. A sentence in an undated Middleton letter to WJJB confirms that it was he who enrolled WJJB as a member of the society. 'The Photographic Society met on Friday night and I enroled you as a member and paid five shillings – eighteen members have joined and there appears every chance of success – I am one of the Committee – therefore can tell you of our proceedings.'

Geology was another shared interest. Middleton in his March 1854 letter writing about their visit to Suffolk wrote, 'I am in debt some crag specimens which I must procure and I think you will be interested in visiting the different places on the Coast'. Botany was another subject that drew the two men together. 'I succeeded in obtaining a rare fern – the ?Castxxx(?) from Surlingham and have potted a plant for you, that you may know it if you succeed in finding it at Edgefield Heath near Holt. I shall be glad to hear you have found it as the localities are not numerous.' This was in one of the Middleton letters; he then continued, 'I am serious by contemplating a greenhouse and fernery.' WJJB had quite clearly been passing on to Middleton his knowledge on the heating of greenhouses, which he had himself learnt from his brilliant cousin Johnson Jex.

Photograph by WJJB of a typical Middleton composition.

Top: Sheringham Park pencil drawing with white highlight 'JM 1852'.

Bottom: 'WJJB 1849 Sheringham Sept 25 Park'. Pencil drawing with white highlight.

The 1854 and 1855 letters, both written in March, give a strong indication of Middleton's fragile health. 'I have been confined to the house for some time..........I presume your intended visit to Lynn would only be an exploring one – as I could not undertake to sketch so early in the spring – my sciatica troubles me – and one of my lungs being very tender I am ordered to be unusually careful.' (March 1854), and the following year, 'As you express a wish about my health...I am much the same...not at all inclined for a journey to the south at present – tho' I ought to go – but I hope in about a fortnight to make up my mind to go to Ventnor – Isle of Wight – at present nothing settled. Can't stand 4½ hours of bumping – there would be nothing left of me.'

Part of John Middleton's letter to WJJB undated, but either 1854 or 1855.

Maybe it was due to his consumption and his poor health that Middleton never married. By the summer of 1856 his illness had become a great trial to him. On 7th October he wrote his Will, and a codicil six days later. On 11th November he died, a brilliant talent snuffed out at the age of twenty-nine. The obituary notice that appeared in the *Norwich Mercury* four days later spoke highly of his personal qualities as well as his artistic ability.

That WJJB and Middleton were good friends there is no doubt. Certainly Middleton's visits to stay with the Bolding family at Weybourne were fulfilling moments in his life. Two of his letters end with sincere messages: 'Remember me to all at home who I hope are well'; and again, 'Remember me kindly to all'.

Middleton's death didn't end the strong link between the two families. WJJB's nephew Francis William (Frank) Monement was not born when Middleton died, but when he went to Norwich School as a boarder in the early 1870s, after his mother had died, his letters to his aunt Hannah back in Weybourne show that he went and visited Mrs Middleton, the artist's stepmother on a number of occasions: 'I went to dinner last Tuesday with Mrs Middleton. I enjoyed it very much. I went for a drive with her.' Again, 'I went to Mrs Middleton today and found her at home for a wonder.' On another occasion he took her some eggs as a present that he had brought from Weybourne.

Norfolk river scene. c1855. (Norfolk County Council).

One more reference to the Middleton family occurred in 1883. Mrs Middleton, the artist's stepmother had died, and there was a two-day sale of items from his studio on 13th and 14th June 1883. In Norwich Castle is an annotated copy of the catalogue of the sale. In pencil are the names of all the purchasers, and prices realised. WJJB was at the auction and bid successfully for seven lots: two oil paintings, 'A Welsh Gate' by A.Gilbert and 'Woods at Weybourne' by John Middleton, and one watercolour of 'Dahlias' by John Middleton. Also four assorted lots: 'Sketches for pictures – four of Weybourne'; 'eight sketches'; 'three sketching books, containing pencil sketches'; 'sketch book, containing sketches by JM, taken in the Isle of Arran'. It is likely that WJJB, concerning the sketches, will have wanted items that had nostalgic connections with Middleton. Does this mean that they might have been together on Middleton's sketching trip to Arran in 1853? Or did WJJB just admire Middleton's large oil of the Isle of Arran, exhibited at the British Institution in London in 1854, which he must have seen closely while it was being painted? WJJB did not buy Lot 399, the description of which was: 'nine etchings – Crome, Bolding etc'. Good company indeed.

John Middleton etching not in his book of nine etchings. In the early 1970s Alec Cotman, the then Assistant Keeper of Art at Norwich Castle, was shown this print by Derick Mellor. In pencil. Cotman wrote, 'note made of this print in the NCM.MS Cat. of etchings'.

Chapter 6

Weybourne – Village People and Tradesmen

The 1851 Census return shows us that there were fourteen fishermen in Weybourne – no surprise as the village was so near the sea, with the fishing boats launched from off the beach. There were thirty-eight agricultural labourers registered in the Census, most of them employed on the land of the Lord of the Manor, the Earl of Orford, or by the Bolding family. The Coastguard Cottages on the beach were occupied by the families of Lieutenant William Thomas and his five officers, none of whom local men. Trades and professions in the village were varied, as one would expect from a small community needing to be as nearly self sufficient as possible. Communications with the outside world were not easy and the railway would not come for more than thirty years into the future. There was a cattle dealer, a blind coal carter, a thatcher, a Sunday School teacher, a shoe binder, a shepherd, two blacksmiths, a rat catcher,

FISH CART

This drawing was among the Bolding family papers in Weybourne. In the first part of the 19th century this cart was no unusual sight in Norfolk. The Fish Carts carried fish from the coastal villages to Norwich and other towns, and the bold notice on the side was to ensure that there would be no unnecessary delay if inspection should be required at any toll gate, particularly in warm weather.

Crown and Anchor Street, Weybourne. Part of the pub sign can be seen behind the cottage on the right. WJJB brown wash drawing from the late 1840s.

a gamekeeper, a dressmaker and a needle-woman. WJJB owned the two public houses in the village. The Crown and Anchor, only a stone's throw across the street from 'The House' (known as Crown and Anchor Street in those days), had as licensee Mr Rowland. He was in trade as a carpenter. Down the street, near the parish church was The Ship. Its licensee, Mr Pilch, was a master-tailor employing an apprentice. WJJB's watermill down Beach Road was operated by Henry Bugden, while the newly built tower mill at the top of the hill on the Sheringham road was owned by John Dawson of Church Street, who farmed fifty acres and was in trade as a miller and maltster employing two labourers.

Five paupers were recorded in the census. If families were really not able to provide for themselves they were likely to be committed to the workhouse. From the last year of the reign of Elizabeth I, the Poor Law Act (1601) had placed the maintenance of the poor onto each individual parish. It was the Poor Law Amendment Act of 1834 that saw workhouses being built to service groups of parishes. The Erpingham Union workhouse at West Beckham (referred to this day as 'The Palace') covered forty-nine parishes, including Weybourne, and had room for three hundred inmates. On 2nd April 1838 John Bolding, WJJB's father, became a Guardian of that workhouse, as his grandson William Bolding Monement would also become in the last years of the century.

Unknown men c 1855

Unknown man. c1855. (Norfolk County Council).

THE SCHOOL CHILDREN

The provenance of this photograph by WJJB is far from clear. His sister Esther in her journal recorded that before her marriage in 1845 she had taught local girls in a private school in Weybourne. WJJB was not taking photographs until well into the 1850's. Is this Mrs Digby with her charges at a later date, or is it after 1875 of pupils at the Board School at Kelling where WJJB was the first Chairman of Governors?

In the 1851 Census Mrs Harriet Digby and Mrs Sarah Grice were described as 'schoolmistresses', with their children as 'scholars at home'. What of education in the village? Shortly before her marriage, WJJB's sister Esther recorded in her journal that she was doing some teaching to local girls in a school founded by a Mrs Chastbury whose daughter Mrs Digby was the teacher. The school started in 1844 and the Reverend Cremer had set the syllabus, the children only being taught to write, spell, read and repeat hymns. WJJB's mother had a far sighted aim that the children should be taught accounts and how to handle money, with the remark, 'Oh, how I hope that the school will succeed. It could so benefit the poor if these girls are taught better ways of doing things.

In a village like Weybourne the corn harvest was the highlight of the year, the gathering in of the barley being the culmination of a whole year's efforts. This began with the ploughing of the fields by the heavy horses the previous autumn. North Norfolk near to the coast has always grown good quality malting barley, and this will have helped WJJB's Weybourne Brewery make good quality beer. In the photograph, the men at the edge of the field, with their scythes at the ready, are preparing to start mowing the field, but first their employer must photograph them for posterity. The woman on the right in her bonnet will too be part of the harvesting. It was the job of the women to bundle up the corn into sheaves, to be set up into stooks, keeping the corn as dry as possible, until being carted. The elaborate precautions by women to keep the sun from their faces reflected the 19th century view that skin browned by the sun was unbecoming. Hannah Beatrice Monement's watercolour (*below*) shows the last of the sheaves being cleared with a man raking some loose straw. In WJJB's splendid oil painting (*next page*) judging by its height, the stack must be nearly complete; a cart has just arrived for its sheaves to be pitched up to the men who wait. Two ladies from 'The House' are watching the proceedings, one seated propped up against a stook.

The late Cliff Middleton, writing in an article in the October 1977 edition of *Norfolk Fair*, stated that WJJB 'seems to have been deliberately setting out to capture the dress and trades of the people who worked for him'. Whether that was so or not, what is clear is that we are left with a wonderful record of the dress of working village people and trades people from the middle years of the 19th century. Cliff Middleton had also stated that 'these are almost certainly the first photographs of Norfolk people ever taken and certainly one of the earliest (comprehensive) photographic records of rural

A splendid photograph from the early 1870s.

A Hannah Beatrice watercolour from the late 1870s, of men gathering in the stooks of barley from a field opposite 'The House'.

WJJB oil painting of a harvest scene
overlooking the priory church in Weybourne.
The recently built tower mill is in the distance.
Signed WJJB and dated 1854.

dress and trades taken anywhere in the world'.

Nearly all the best of WJJB's photographic portraits of the village people were taken in his studio, the upstairs room the whole length of the
barn only a stone's throw from 'The House'. The canvas backdrop is there,
with occasionally the mottled carpet showing. Often the clothes of the sitters hide the chair that was so often used.

The names of a few of the village people are recorded, but most are
unknown. Only one person, who worked for WJJB for over forty years,
can be followed through from his birth in 1832 to his death in 1917, with
details of his own family.

William Cook(e) was born on 12th January 1832 and was christened
three days later. His father John, an agricultural labourer (stated in the
1841 Census), and mother Elizabeth were both twenty-one years old
when they married in 1830. In the 1851 Census the family name was now
spelt 'Cooke', with John recorded as a farm steward. William, aged nineteen, described as an agricultural labourer, was still living at home. (The
'Cooke' spelling appears on all census forms through until the 1901 Census when it reverts to 'Cook'). On 24th February 1857 William (aged twen-

ty-four) married Frances Field (aged nineteen) from Kelling, the next door village to Weybourne, in Kelling church. The christening of a daughter Mary is shown as taking place on 27th November 1859. In the 1861 Census William is now a 'jobbing gardener', presumably working part time for WJJB. From the 1871 Census he is recorded as a 'gardener', now working full time for WJJB and living in the cottage immediately opposite to 'The House'. His father John died in 1878, and the 1881 Census has Elizabeth Cooke, aged 72, described as a bread seller (baker), living with her son and daughter-in-law. Mary was now twenty-one and a dressmaker, an occupation that appeared on all subsequent census returns.

Rose Cooke, aged five, is on that census. Was she really a very late surprise for Frances (now nearly forty), or was she taken in by the family for some reason unknown and given the family name? Twenty years on in the 1901 Census she is there, aged twenty-five. William Cook (yes, now not 'Cooke'), aged sixty-nine, was no longer 'gardener' in the 1901 Census, but a Parish Worker. His former employer had died eighteen months before.

William Cook(e) WJJB's gardener for over forty years with his daughter Mary. c1864.

Rose Cooke married William Finney, who was born in Staffordshire, in 1906 and they went to live in North Walsham, fifteen miles away. William Cooke's wife Frances died in 1906. By the 1911 Census William, with his daughter Mary, were living in Bodham, two miles from Weybourne, and he was described as 'Parish Clerk'. At his death he was seventy-nine years old. Mary lived on until 1936 when she died aged seventy-seven.

William Cook(e) as an older man. 1880s.

Chapter 7

Family and Friends

Dating WJJB's photographs is not an easy task. Certainly some of the portraits of the village people were exhibited in Norwich in 1856, and a number of other classic examples date into the 1860s. A small number of family photographs are earlier than 1857. The dates of birth and death of all the family members are known, so the task of dating can be judged by assessing the age of the sitter / sitters. WJJB's mother, 'Old' Esther, comes across as being a formidable lady; none of the photographs of his unmarried sister Hannah show her in a flattering light; she was no beauty, unlike her sister Esther. It is the photographs of 'Young' Esther, her husband William and their nine surviving children that are of great interest.

That the Boldings and the Monements were a close family unit must be so, because from the early days up to WJJB's death in 1899, there are many threads running through to support this. The census returns from the middle of the century are of considerable interest. In 1851 Hannah Bolding was in King's Lynn with her sister

Esther Bolding wearing a fine example of a Norwich shawl, which would have been deep terracotta red in colour. c1860.

WJJB's mother Esther Bolding. c1855. She is wearing her best silk dress with sloping shoulders, typical of the 1850s. Her lace bonnet and different ribbons around her neck help indicate that she, though an older woman, still had great dress sense.

and brother-in-law, three very small children and two living-in female servants. 1861 is more revealing. Resident in King's Lynn is Hannah with four nieces and a nephew, aged from 10 years to 10 months, helped by a cook, housekeeper and a nursemaid. In Weybourne are William and Esther, with the two eldest boys, staying with WJJB and his mother. The servants are recorded as a cook, a housemaid, a house servant and a twelve-year-old house boy.

The photographs of family members were all taken at Weybourne, either in WJJB's studio or outside in one of the gardens. This indicates that family visits to the north Norfolk coast were regular and frequent. There are some wonderful examples surviving. The eldest boy, William Bolding Monement, is rarely seen photographed in a relaxed situation, except when he is holding his gun. In adult life he would become a renowned wild fowler. John Francis Bolding Monement, who was to emigrate to New Zealand at nineteen, was happy to sit for his uncle, and to be photographed with his sisters. Probably one of WJJB's most endearing compositions is of his sister Esther with her four eldest girls and John Francis Bolding Monement taken in the early 1860s (see page 92). Great use is made of props and the whole set up is way ahead of its time. It is stunning. No-one is looking 'wooden', so often the criticism of Victorian photographic portraiture.

A photograph of John Francis Bolding Monement in his mid to later teens shows a serious-minded young man. I looked up 'Cricket Archive' on the internet, thinking that there might be a reference to William Bolding Monement or to Frank Monement, who I knew were

Esther Monement. c1855. Her brightly coloured silk skirt might have been a cobalt blue and yellow in the tartan plaid, using the latest aniline dyes. She certainly was very fashionably dressed.

1 Hannah Bolding, WJJB's unmarried sister. c1855.

2 John Francis Bolding Monement with a red squirrel. c1858.

3 John Francis Bolding Monement. c1861.

4 John Francis Bolding Monement with his sisters Eleanor Bolding and Martha Grace. c1860.

ALL-ENGLAND CRICKET ELEVEN

In the 1840s, the 'Middle Ages' of cricket, after the Hambledon Club of the late 18th century and before the arrival of W.G.Grace in the middle of the 1860s,William Clarke of Nottingham originated and captained the professional All-England Eleven. They played against odds, the opposition normally consisting of eighteen or twenty-two players. H.S.Altham in his *History of Cricket* (1926) described them as 'truly missionaries of cricket' taking the game to all parts of the country, which accelerated its interest and circulation.

By 1852 there was dissent in the ranks, and John Wisden (of the *Cricketer's Almanack*) and others broke away and formed the United England Eleven, which concentrated more in the south of England. After Clarke's death in 1856 the two elevens met each other annually at Lord's,

which was the great match of the season.

The All-England Eleven of 1866 which played against twenty-two of King's Lynn was captained by George Parr. He had been one of the great batsmen for the past twenty years. Both he, and the All-England Eleven, were coming to the end of their time, as 1873, with nine counties, saw the start of the County Championship of First-Class cricket.

In 1866 the All-England Eleven played eighty-eight days cricket between 14th May and 15th September, a punishing schedule indeed. A seventeen-year-old W.G.Grace captained the Nottingham and Sheffield Colts Eighteen which lost to them in a two-day match immediately before their coming to King's Lynn. What W.G., from Gloucestershire, was doing up in the north Midlands, history doesn't relate.

fine sportsmen, only to find that from the 7th to the 9th June 1866, when he was barely seventeen, John Francis Bolding Monement played cricket for twenty-two of King's Lynn against the 'All England XI' in a two innings match (see above). 'J.Monement' batted at number twenty, made one in the first innings and five in the second. On both occasions he was 'b Tilney' (R.C.Tilney (1830-1900) of Nottinghamshire, described as 'underarm slow') who took twenty wickets in the match. The All England XI, from mid May to mid September, toured the northern areas of the country playing mainly three-day matches against town teams, mostly of eighteen or twenty-two players.

It was almost certainly 1869 that John Francis Bolding Monement emigrated to New Zealand, but there are no clues as to why he departed for the other side of the world. He took with him a double-barrel pin fire breech-loading shotgun made between 1857 and 1863, a present from his father or his uncle. This, with the wooden cartridge box, survive: email photographs from Australia, sent by a descendant of his, have provided the evidence. On the box, clearly shown is, 'J.Potter – Gun, Rifle and Pistol Manufacturer – 52 High Street, Lynn'.John Francis Bolding Monement married Mary Cleary of Dunedin, New Zealand who bore him five children. After twenty years the family moved to South Australia, and, finally, for the last sixteen years of his life, to Wollongong in New South Wales, where he died in 1911. I had made contact with descendants in Australia and received a copy of John Francis Bolding Monement's death certificate which provided the information above.

1871 was a dramatic year as Esther had died, aged 50, on 30th March just before the census date. At the family home in King's Lynn, a cousin Hannah Johnson (from Salthouse) was looking after the youngest two girls aged ten and nine. In Weybourne the two boys and two of the girls were with their aunt and uncle, with a cook, housemaid, under maid and boy servant recorded. The widower William Monement and the two eldest girls were at neither address. None of the three appear on the census anywhere, so one presumes that they were abroad.

The death of the mother was certainly a turning point for the family and from then on one has the impression that Weybourne was home as much as King's Lynn, the siblings taking it in turns to support their father who was heavily involved in the affairs of the borough. He had been mayor of Lynn in 1864, and in 1881 was recorded as senior alderman and was still a magistrate. This was five years before he died. When his cork business was sold is not known. It is not clear when the cottage, nearly opposite to 'The House', became a holiday home for the Monement family, and then, in time, a permanent home for the unmarried sisters. The

Top and above: The shotgun taken by John Francis Bolding Monement to New Zealand.

Below: The gun case: J.Potter, 52 High Street, Lynn.

JOHN FRANCIS BOLDING MONEMENT'S EMIGRATION TO NEW ZEALAND – THEN TO AUSTRALIA

I made contact with Monements in Australia nearly ten years ago after finding details on Google. They sent a copy of John Francis Bolding Monement's death certificate in 1911(below). which proved that he will have left England c1869. The photograph of the gentleman sitting cross legged with his shotgun on his lap, his gun dog and game bag at his side was enclosed, with the caption, 'Do you know who this

is?' Well, it is Francis William Monement. He is sitting outside the house he had built in 1900 in Cley, on land he had inherited on the death of his uncle WJJB in 1899. The photograph will have been taken by Rose Monement, who WJJB had taught to be a very proficient photographer, and sent to their brother in Australia. The photographs of the shotgun were emailed from Australia to me.

Frank Monement inherited the Cley estate in 1899 on WJJB's death.

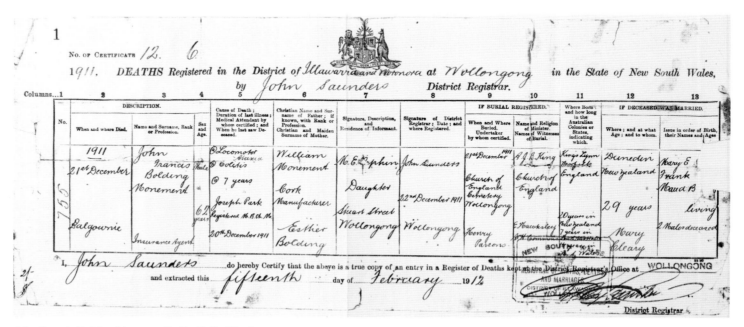

John Francis Bolding Monement's Death Certificate.

Left: An amazing reflective composition. The year is 1871 and the girls' mother has recently died. Of the Monement sisters only Eleanor Bolding (aged 17) is absent. Hannah Beatrice (aged 19) is seated and looking towards the camera, a hand round the family dog. Rose (aged 11) has her left hand resting gently on the dog. Maude Marguerite (aged 10), head bowed, has her right hand resting on Rose's shoulder, and the eldest, Mary Esther (aged 20) has a hand holding Maude Marguerite's right arm for comfort.

Below: An unknown man with the family dog.

earliest photograph shows a small simple cottage, but by the time WJJB had died in 1899 it had been added on to again and again, that it ended up as an eleven bedroom house, but still named 'The Cottage', as the name remained until modern times. The adding on may have started before their mother died, but it is likely that the brothers and sisters spent more and

Three photographs of William Monement in later life.

CROQUET

The earliest record of the use of the word 'croquet' was in the 1850s. In 1868 the All England Croquet Club was formed at Wimbledon, but from the 17th century, during the reign of Charles II, paille-maille or pall mall, derived from the Latin words for 'ball' and 'mallet', had been introduced from France.

The delightful study of three of WJJB's nieces playing croquet will date from the early 1870s when they were in mourning for the death of their mother in 1871. The eldest niece Mary Esther is in the middle, while the youngest, Maude Marguerite, aged twelve or thirteen, is kneeling. The man mowing the croquet lawn is not Billy Cook the gardener.

WIMBLEDON LAWN TENNIS CHAMPIONSHIPS

Real Tennis (or Royal Tennis), played indoors, had been in existence for centuries. Amazingly, it was as late as 1873 that Major Walter Wingfield invented a version of Real Tennis played outdoors on a lawn. 1877 was the first year when Men's Singles were played at the All England Croquet Club at Wimbledon; twenty-two 'Gentlemen' entered and Spencer Gore was the first winner. 1880 was the year when the Monement broth-

Left: William Bolding Monement (on ground) and Francis William Monement. c1880. *Right*: The tennis court near 'The House' with two unnamed girls playing - 1880s.

ers played. O.E.Woodhouse, who beat Frank Monement in four sets in the second round, then beat W.C.Renshaw in the third round and his twin brother J.E.Renshaw in the fourth round, before losing to H.F.Lawford in the final. That year the Renshaws were nineteen years old and one year out of school at Cheltenham College. The Renshaws brought a new dimension to the game, in that they introduced the 'overhead smash'. W.C.Renshaw won the Singles in 1881, and for the following five years, became a household name, and is the first legendary hero in the Wimbledon story. Doubles were played for the first time in 1884, the same year that the Ladies made their first appearance at the championships.

more time thereafter in Weybourne. In 1871 the two oldest girls were twenty and nineteen, with the next two not far behind. In the 1901 census the unmarried sisters, living in 'The Cottage' are described as 'living off own means', so good works in the local community will have been part of their lives. Neither of the two boys had a career and they too 'lived off own means'. William Bolding Monement, as the heir to WJJB's Weybourne estate, certainly lived permanently with his uncle and aunt in 'The

WILLIAM BOLDING MONEMENT AND PUNT GUNNING

An extract from the 1925 obituary for William Bolding Monement printed in the *Norfolk Chronicle*:

As a wildfowler I believe he divided the honours with Sir Ralph Payne-Gallwey of being probably the greatest living authority in England. How many a night he has been out at Blakeney after duck, temperature below freezing. At one time he and some friends used to go to Holland, and they got enough duck and

William Bolding Monement as a teenager with his first gun. c1860

other wildfowl which, when sold at Leadenhall Market, nearly paid for their expenses. But this was not very long allowed, the authorities raising the cost of the licence to such a pitch that Leadenhall no longer paid the expenses.

The art of punt shooting, broadly speaking, consists of the fowler's ability, firstly, whilst lying concealed on the floor of his punt, to propel his craft stealthily within gunshot of a number of wild fowl, and secondly, so accurately to judge his distance, aim, and fire his gun, as to bag the largest number, whether there be many or few birds to shoot at. Two groups of people from the opposite ends of the social scale carried out punt gunning: those who had to do it to help them make a living (market gunners), and those who had sufficient money that they did not have to work (gentlemen gunners)' from *The Encyclopedia of Sports and Games* 1911.

The market gunners obviously did not like the gentlemen gunners as they affected their living. Monement, a gentleman gunner, seems to have punted on his own, that is he used a single handed punt, but was often accompanied by another gentle-

William Bolding Monement's wild fowling journal illustrating page 208 – part of '1891: Four and a half days at Blakeney' (see page 164).

man gunner using another punt outfit.

Monement's wildfowling journal started in 1880 with 'A Punting Trip to Holland' when he was thirty-four years old. The journal, in a hardback morocco bordered exercise book, recorded other trips to Holland: 1881 (2), 1882 (2), 1886, 1888; to Fairlie, Scotland 1883; Tiree, Southern Hebrides 1884; Oban and Tiree 1885 – as well as the two Blakeney expeditions, 1891 and 1898. On his overseas trips he always took a companion (three Upchers from Sheringham Hall are recorded: Hannay, Edward and Hamilton, as well as a George Creswell). To Holland he was often away for almost a month (1881: 596 fowl in 27 days).

Four photographs of Francis William (Frank) Monement, as a very small boy, as a teenager and as a young adult. He was my late wife Pauline's grandfather and he died a year before she was born.

1. c1862.

2. c1863.

3. c1872, in his Norwich School uniform.

4. c1882, in his Norfolk jacket and matching trousers.

House' after his father's death in 1886, maybe even before that time. He became involved in many good works locally, though how early is not recorded. He was on the Erpingham Rural District Council, the Weybourne Parish Council, the Board of Guardians of the Erpingham Union Workhouse at West Beckham, and Chairman of Kelling School Managers for thirty years. (As a result of the 1870 Education Act for compulsory education, the Board School was founded at Kelling in 1875 with WJJB as its first chairman. William Bolding Monement clearly took over when his uncle stood down.)

It was as a sportsman that William Bolding Monement excelled. His obituarist in the *Norfolk Chronicle* in 1925 wrote, 'I do not know of his equal in the county'. He was in the Christ's College, Cambridge cricket eleven in 1865 and 'won many of the events in athletics'; he was fond of boxing and 'boxed many boxers of repute'; he 'excelled in revolver shoot-

All six Monement sisters with their brother Frank, in the front garden of 'The Cottage'. c1880 (William Bolding Monement was probably away on one of his wildfowling expeditions).

ing and yearly went to Wimbledon (modern Bisley) always winning many prizes'. In the 1870s he 'took to lawn tennis and rapidly achieved greatness going with his brother Frank to Wimbledon.' This they did in 1880, the third year of the All England Championships. Both lost in the second round, Frank Monement (age 22) to the losing finalist O.E. Woodhouse and William Bolding Monement (age 34) to H.F. Lawford, the Singles Champion. He also played a good game of bowls, but his great love was for shooting. The obituary went overboard, as quoted on page 128.

Frank Monement's education can be followed through family letters that are now in my possession. In 1868 he was aged ten when his mother wrote to him at Downham (Downham Market) where he was living with the Miss Mumford sisters, who must have been his governesses. After his mother's death in 1871 he was sent to Norwich School. Over twenty letters written by him from school to his aunt Hannah Bolding back in Weybourne survive. The early ones have the paper edged in black, in mourning for his mother, the later ones on notepaper with the school crest at the top with handwritten 'School House' underneath. Clearly Weybourne is central to his thoughts. He asks after people in the village, sometimes inquiring after some in poor health. Keeping budgerigars and other birds was a keen hobby, and he asks after his pets. (He bought and sold birds in Norwich.) On occasions a hamper of food from Weybourne is requested.

Three letters show that Frank went on to Cirencester Agricultural College, so after that he may have been some help to his uncle, in the latter's declining years, with the running of the farms. Mention of cricket, tennis, boxing, fives and shooting show that he was also clearly an all-round sportsman, but his achievements are not so well documented as those of his brother. As a young adult he certainly enjoyed posing for the camera; he is caught sitting crossed-legged on a low stool playing a banjo; in a photograph taken about 1880, in the garden of 'The Cottage' with his six sisters, he is leaning nonchalantly against the ivy-covered flint wall. Apart from a few photographs that include John Francis Bolding Monement, WJJB's nieces were much more amenable for him to organise studio photographic sessions with them. From young ages he had them dressing up. There is a lovely shot of one of the girls wearing what may well be a tartan skirt far too big for her, with an adult shawl draped over her head, hanging down almost to the ground. On her left arm, tucked against her side, is a small wicker basket. In another, one of the girls is made to look like a young soldier, standing, with the musket on her right side almost as tall as the top of the cavalry style helmet she is wearing. There are several situations where there are little playlets in two or three photographs. In one, two sisters are seated facing the camera. In the first scene they are clearly in disagreement. In the second, serious efforts are beingmade to settle things; and in the third, they have made up and both are happy.

Mary Esther Monement. c1857.

Mary Esther Monement. c1858. Mary Esther was WJJB's eldest niece, and probably a favourite too. She was certainly photographed more extensively than any others of his family. Here are two of her, described above, having gone to the dressing up cupboard. There are images of family members dressing up, and acting, over a period of more than twenty-five years. Most likely by the 1880s Rose Monement was taking the photographs of these 'performances'.

A three part acting scene.Titles for each could be:
1. 'Falling out';
2. 'Trying to make up',
3. 'All's well again'.. c1875.

Another little playlet, in an outdoor scene, has a courtier and his lady seated. Then a knavish person is seen peeping through a gap in the curtain, and, finally, the courtier is dead on the ground with the distraught lady standing over him (see photographs page 142).

By the 1881 Census all the nephews and nieces were grown up. Three of the girls were with their father in King's Lynn, while the other three were in Weybourne with their uncle and aunt. It is clear that the nieces, when they were adults, often spent time in the company of non family friends, especially in the summer months when families came to Weybourne for their holidays. Some photographs from the late 1870s onwards have non family members included, which makes me more uncertain about identification. One family, the Hamonds, can be directly identified. The Monement family albums have photographs of Chenda (Richenda) Hamond (born 1862), one year younger than Maude Marguerite, the youngest Monement girl, and one presumes they were good friends. Nearly ten years ago I saw a Hamond family journal in which it is stated that in 1883 Chenda had 'a happy month in Weybourne'. It seems clear that several families homed in on Weybourne in the summerholiday season and spent time together. There is a delightful photograph of Maude Marguerite Monement, Chenda Hamond and three other unknown girls of a similar age (erroneously declared by me as five of WJJB's nieces when illustrating an article on WJJB over ten years ago for the Blakeney Area History Society). The girls are sitting on a low flint wall outside a house in

Richenda (Chenda) Hamond, on holiday in Weybourne. She was a good friend of Maude Marguerite Monement, and was photographed, most likely by Rose Monement, outside 'The Cottage'. c1882.

Weybourne. A black labrador, with its hind legs on the ground, has its front paws on the lap of the girl on the left. Three of the other four girls have small dogs on their laps. Maude Marguerite Monement, with a crucifix round her neck, is second from the right and the only family member in the photograph, which most likely was taken by Rose Monement (*right*).

Maude Marguerite Monement, second right, with four friends on holiday in Weybourne. c1882.

In much more recent times the Hamond connection in Weybourne in Victorian times has been fully revealed. Robert Hamond (1809-83), from August 1832 to May 1833, was first mate of H.M.S. *Beagle*, the 10 gun brig-sloop, captained by Lieut. Robert FitzRoy (1805-65), later Vice-Admiral Fitzroy, and pioneering meteorologist, that made history by having Charles Darwin (1809-82) on board, on their way to the Galapagos Islands in the Pacific Ocean. By 1840 the same Robert Hamond was manager of Gurney's Bank in Fakenham, Norfolk and living in a large house in the town. In late middle age he built himself a house in Weybourne as a holiday home, and for his retirement later.

Chenda was his niece, so there were obviously considerable gatherings of Hamond young in Weybourne in the summer months. It was a mag-

The house in Weybourne built by Robert Hamond as a holiday/retirement home. He is seen on the balcony with a telescope to his eye looking out to sea. 1860s.

Charles Darwin (1809-82) from a *Carte de Visite* found in a Hamond family album.

ical day when I tracked down a photograph of Robert Hamond taken by WJJB in a Hamond family album. It dates probably from the middle 1860s and is a fine portrait. Also discovered was a WJJB photograph of Robert Hamond's newly-built house in Weybourne (*previous page*). When Charles Darwin died in 1882 Robert Hamond was the only survivor from

Hannah Beatrice Monement (seated) and probably Mary Esther Monement standing. c1868

the historic *Beagle* voyage present at his funeral in St Paul's Cathedral.

In the Hamond family photograph album is a portrait of a 'Dr Vaughan', in clerical dress, so he must be Revd. Vaughan D.D. It has all the marks of being a WJJB photograph, and this is proven by there being an identical copy in one of our family photograph collections. Many friends of WJJB's

Hannah Beatrice Monement and Mary Esther Monement playing chess. c1868

Robert Hamond (1809–83). c1860 (Hamond family album).

1 'Dr Vaughan' Revd Vaughan D.D. c1860 A photograph of this gentleman is in the family collection, and one was found in a Hamond family album.

2 An unknown clergyman friend of the family. c1855.

4 Unknown man. c1855.

3 An unknown friend of the family. c1860.

family visiting 'The House' were persuaded to cross the yard to the barn, and to the upstairs studio, to have their image taken for posterity; yet so many are anonymous and unknown. The Upchers at Sheringham Hall were clearly good friends and one wonders if any of them are among the photographs that survive.

A common thread through the upbringing and development of WJJB's nephews and nieces was that through his own skills and interests, and his obvious great personality, I have been able to identify how far and wide-ranging were some of their skills, over which he must have been a huge influence. Hannah Beatrice Monement has left behind several albums of her watercolours; not a huge amount of talent, but pleasing to the eye. Some of hers of Weybourne scenes complement those drawn by her uncle half a generation before. Rose Cicely Monement became a very proficient photographer, and from the early 1880s onwards care has to be taken before stating that WJJB took a particular photograph. She certainly took the only sizeable photographic portrait of WJJB surviving, taken towards the end of the 1880s; he is standing in his garden walking stick in hand (see page 83).

The four nieces who never married became very skilled at wood turning, so much so that there are several examples of their work in the village to this day. The most important are the poppy heads at the ends of the pews in Weybourne church (*opposite*), numbering over fifty, which were copied from the few medieval ones still to be seen in the church. In 'The Cottage' there is ('was' if the property developer in the 21st century pulled it out) an amazing floor to ceiling fireplace surround that the nieces made. 'The House' and another residence in the village have examples of their work. There may be more. The two boys inherited a love of fishing, which had been recorded as an interest of WJJB's in his younger days. In William Bolding Monement's obituary it was stated that 'his fingers were nimble and he was a good carpenter. He built more than one boat for wild-fowl shooting.'

By the 1891 Census, both WJJB and his sister Hannah were feeling their age and were in poor health. William Bolding Monement, heir to WJJB's Weybourne estate, was at 'The House' with his uncle and aunt.

Maude Marguerite Monement, probably photographed by her sister Rose. 1880s.

Top: The poppy heads at the ends of the church pews in Weybourne was the work of WJJB's four unmarried nieces. The three memorials to the family can be seen on the north wall in the chancel. c1995.

Bottom: The memorials to WJJB and his family on the north wall of the chancel in Weybourne church.

There was a nurse living in, as well as a cook and two housemaids. Across the road in 'The Cottage' were Martha Grace Monement and Ellinor Bolding Monement, both 'living off her own means', with a cook and a domestic housemaid. Hannah Beatrice Monement had married Edgar Goble, a

Unknown man, with his brand new Penny Farthing, probably photographed by Rose Monement. 1880s.

solicitor from Fareham, Hampshire the previous year, and they, with their first child, were recorded in Fareham in the census. Maude Marguerite Monement, the youngest of the six girls, would marry Frederick Bowden-Smith later in that census year. She is not recorded in the census, so must have been abroad, as too were Mary Esther Monement and Rose Cicely Monement, as well as her brother Frank Monement.

Hannah Beatrice Monement clutching her doll, while her sister Martha Grace stares intently at hers propped up on a chair.

The Third Eleven
– and more

It was decided to have only a small number of 'dressing up' and 'acting' photographs to support the text in the book. Looking at the remainder, it became clear that there were more that deserved to be included; hence the idea of a 'Third Eleven' evolved, but it ended up as more than eleven photographs. Cricket followers will identify with my 'team' thinking. The 'Second Eleven' went into bat first, as the 'First Eleven' was always going to be placed near the middle of the book.

As has been stated before, WJJB's eldest niece Mary Esther Monement was his most photogenic family model, and a series of images of her through her early years are included here.

'The Banquet' and the other strange photograph on page 149 really bring home to us in the 21st century that young adults in the later Victorian period, from well to do backgrounds, found much pleasure and satisfaction from 'dressing up' and 'acting'. It enlivened their often mundane lives.

The photographs on page 150 remind us of WJJB's powers of composition: the use of hands, elbows and arms, and the angles of his sitters' heads, which all draw one into the images.

The Naval cadet

(Norfolk County Council)

Murder Most Foul!

Mary Esther Monement c1861

More of Mary Esther

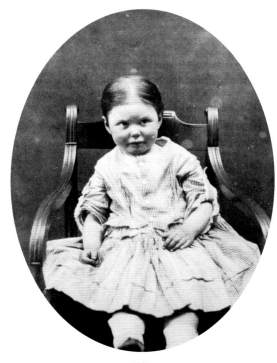

Mary Esther Monement and Hannah Beatrice Monement in their travelling coats.

Chess can be very tiring! (See also two of their sisters playing chess on page 135)

Top: Frank Monement, in a sailor's uniform, is standing, left, while his brother Wiliam Bolding is in a GER (Great Eastern Railway) uniform towards the right. Three sisters and three non-family friends are seated. The photograph is most probably taken by Rose Monement c1882.

Bottom: The only comment that can be made about this photograph, probably taken by Rose Monement, is that her sister Mary Esther is seated second right!

149

Postscript

Much of the land that for the nearly two hundred years WJJB, his ancestors and descendants, held in Weybourne was copyhold from either the Waborne Manor Court or the Waborne Priory Manor Court. The first recorded evidence of family landholding was in 1748 when WJJB's great great grandfather William Jennis was admitted at the Manor Court to 'an estate at Waborne – dwelling house, malthouse etc'. In 1936 Frank Monement, WJJB's nephew, who had inherited the Weybourne estate in 1925 on the death of his brother William Bolding Monement, paid compensation of £1140 to the Countess of Orford, the Lord of the Manor, whereby the copyhold land became freehold. Frank Monement died in 1943, with 'The House' having been requisitioned by the army as an officers mess for the military camp at Muckleburgh during the Second World War. In 1946 'The House' was sold by Frank's widow, Olivia, and was sold on the following year as the Maltings hotel. By the end of the 1950s all the family land and property in Weybourne had been sold.

Now, in the 21st century, the new owners of Priory Farm, to the north of the religious buildings in Weybourne, in conjunction with English Heritage, have restored the monastic cloisters and other ruined remains. It is almost as though the wheel has turned full circle because the priory ruins and parish church were quite clearly a consuming passion for WJJB. Inside the church, on a wall facing the south door entrance, is a brass plaque inscribed as follows: 'BY REQUEST OF W.J.J.BOLDING OF THIS PARISH, THE NAVE OF THIS CHURCH WAS RESEATED AND REFLOORED, THUS COMPLETING THE WORK BEGUN BY HIM DURING HIS LIFETIME. JUNE 22 1902'. It is quite clear that the inside of the church, as we see it now, is largely due to the benefaction of WJJB.

For fourteen years I 'commuted' by car from my home in Cley next the Sea to my teaching job in West Runton, just east of Sheringham, daily passing through Weybourne. On the return journey the c1850 tower mill signalled the descent into Weybourne village, coming down past the church; on the bend, on the left, is the Ship public house, then the former Gashe's Restaurant, so loved by many in the 1950s and 1960s; on a straight piece of road is the Maltings hotel on the right and then almost opposite it, 'The Cottage', now divided up. Immediately past it on a low wall is a sign: 'BOLDING WAY', leading to houses down a drive. The name lives on.

Two buildings that I have not identified. I thought that the crenellated building was the gatehouse to Baconsthorpe Castle, four miles or so from Weybourne, but it proved not to be.

Appendix I

W.J.J. Bolding the Archaeologist

On the sheet with plans of Weybourne priory in the Norwich Record Office WJJB stated quite clearly that 1830 was the year in which he actively became interested in the archaeology of the priory ruins and the parish church. He was fourteen years old. He drew these plans in 1891; at the bottom of the document it states: 'W.J.J.Bolding – Waborne 1830 to 1891', so recording sixty-one years of study on the ruins. A remarkable record indeed.

The Norfolk and Norwich Archaeological Society was founded in 1846. WJJB doesn't seem to have been elected a member until well into the 1850s, which is surprising as he was active with his archaeology before the end if the 1840s. In 1849 there was a Lynn meeting of the Society when Henry Harrod, first joint Honorary Secretary of the Society, led an excursion to Castle Rising castle four miles from King's Lynn. The rectangular keep is a fine example of a mid-12th-century Norman fortification, similar in style to the castle that dominates the Norwich skyline. WJJB was certainly on the excursion because he sketched views of the castle. Two that survive are dated August 1849. This was the beginning of the story, because Harrod wrote extensively on

'WJJB Aug 8 1849 Castle Rising'. Pencil drawings, with white highlight, of the gatehouse and entrance to the castle (right) and the keep in the bailey (left).

Etched by H.Ninham

GATE HOUSE & BRIDGE. CASTLE RISING.

N O R F O L K.

'Etched by H.Ninham Gate house and bridge, Castle Rising, Norfolk', WJJB Aug 1849 can clearly be seen in the bottom left-hand corner.

his findings which were published in book form: *Documents relating to Castle Rising with notices of the past and present state of the building* printed by Charles Muskett, Old Haymarket MDCCCLII (1852). On page 70 is an etching by Henry Ninham, the Norwich School artist of 'THE GATE HOUSE & BRIDGE, CASTLE RISING. NORFOLK'. WJJB's initials and the August 1849 date are quite clearly seen at the bottom left-hand corner, so Ninham etched from his drawing. Volume IV of Norfolk Archaeology, published in 1855, has an article of Harrod's Castle Rising excursion, with WJJB's Ninham etching.

One fascinating item of WJJB's that does survive is a large artist's sketchbook. There are eight pencil and brown monochrome drawings of Weybourne, three dated in 1849, followed by one page, dated April 23 1866, of a pen/grey wash drawing of two Bronze Age spear heads, and another archaeological drawing. Turn the book round and at the other end are eight more pencil and brown monochrome drawings of Weybourne, one dated 1849. There then follows eleven pages under the initial heading: 'Archaeological Society'. In the left-hand margin are a few dates (November 1849 to 1851) and single words indicating individual expeditions. Then his notes.

Nov. 1849　　*Having requested H.Harrod Esq, Our hon. Sec, to pay me a visit the following are minutes and observations arising from my connection with the society.*

Nov.12　　*Monday Mr Harrod after looking at the priory pits and tumuli on Salthouse Common thinks they are all interesting and worthy of notice – the pits he says are Celtic.*

Slag　　*I have found some slag at Waborne. The same as that found at Felbrigg and Beeston he (Mr Harrod) thinks there is no doubt about its being the remains of beacon fires. I question it.*
See letters Dec.14 & 29 [18]49.

Jany 1850　　*I have been making a map of the pits. There are about*

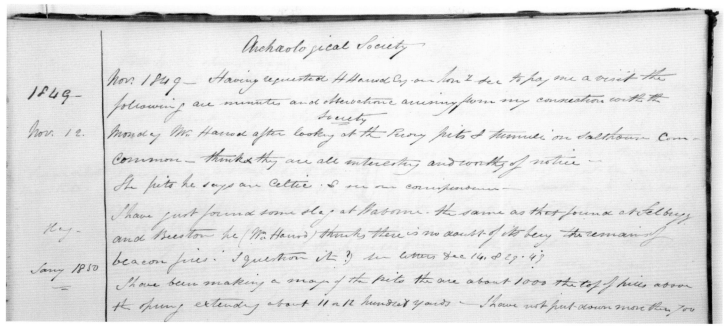

1000 of the hills above ... extending about 11 or 12 hundred yards – have not put down more than 700. (This was the basis for H.Ninham's lithograph, the illustration supporting Henry Harrod's article in Norfolk Archaeology Volume III (1852) pages 232-240: "On the Weybourne Pits").

March	We have just opened one of the Salthouse tumuli. It is right of the road leading from Salthouse.
Salthouse	to the Lowes. Beginning to cut from the NE to centre. Just at the beginning we found a vase
Common	but nothing in the centre except charcoal mixed with the earth for about 5 feet in depth and twenty yards or nearly so in width covered with a thick layer of large gravel stones.

'Archaeological Society Nov. 1849 ...' The beginning of several pages of archaeological notes (and drawings) by WJJB concerning various excavations he and others undertook on behalf of the Norfolk and Norwich Archaeological Society, mainly near Weybourne.

WJJB and Henry Harrod clearly worked together on many occasions and must have been good friends and he was central to WJJB's involvement with the Norwich circle.

Slag, from the notes in WJJB's observations, was quite clearly his prime target with his involvement with local archaeology. 'Slag pits' and

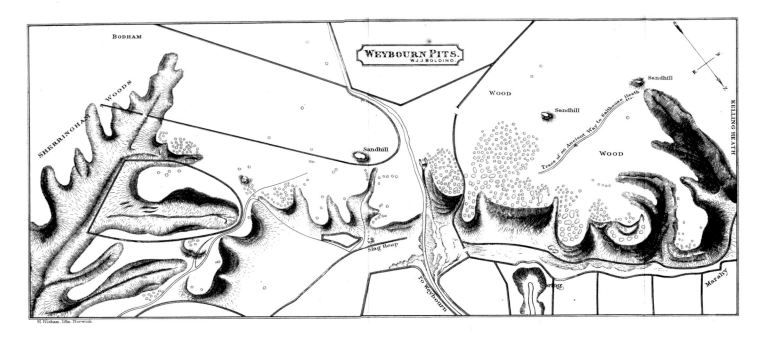

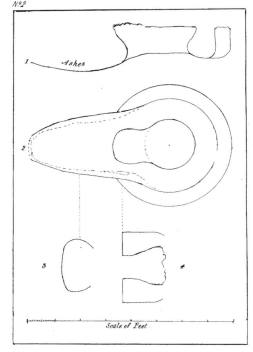

Above: A Lithograph by the Norwich School artist Henry Ninham, from 'a plan by W.J.J.Bolding', that supported the article 'On the Weybourne Pits' by Henry Harrod, published in Norfolk Archaeology Vol.III, 1852 (see page 160).

Left: 'Sketch of the Weybourne Pits', signed 'H.H. 1850'. A print accompanying Henry Harrod's article in Norfolk Archaeology Vol.III (see page 160).

Right: Plan and section of the 'Ancient Potter's Kiln' excavated by WJJB which appeared in Norfolk Archaeology Vol.V, 1859 (see page 161).

SKETCH OF THE WEYBOURNE PITS.

1. *Section of the Kiln.*   3. *Section of the fire place.*

2. *Plan of the Do.*   4. *Do. of the flue & table.*

156

'slag heaps' appear again and again. Slag is the waste from iron that has been worked and mostly indicated workings from the Iron Age. WJJB's interest stemmed from his desire to understand how man in earlier times lived. Apart from his workings in Weybourne, mainly on the high ground above the village on what is now the edge of Kelling Heath, he was slag pit hunting, and tumuli hunting, further afield. His notes have him digging at Beeston Regis (beyond Sheringham), at Edgefield (beyond Holt), and at Cawston, Buxton and Horstead, all on the way towards Norwich.

A wonderfully evocative grey wash drawing of two gentlemen archaeologists digging with their spades – intending to represent WJJB and Mr Chester (Revd Greville Chester) at Horstead Feb 25 1851.

There is a brown wash drawing of a whole urn found on Salthouse Common, measuring 13 inches across the rim and 6 inches across the base. It is below writing on a barrow which 'was opened by Mr G Chester Aug. 1850. I was with him on the second day. It is marked on the map no ... and is ... feet in diameter and five in height and there is no appearance of a ditch or......was not quite as many stones and burnt earth as we found in no ... the perfect urn was found near the centre and fragments of two more ... they were much broken and only three pieces of no.3 We opened a barrow by cutting a trench across no. but found nothing except burnt earth and charcoal no stones.' (WJJB clearly excavated a number of the round barrows up on Salthouse Heath, and of course to modern archaeologists, did untold damage with his primitive excavations).

On the next page in the book is a drawing and underneath an explanation of the exploit:

Revd Greville John Chester (1830–92)

His father was rector of Denton in Norfolk. Greville developed a passionate interest in antiquities from childhood. When he was seventeen he wrote a paper on Roman remains in Norfolk, and while still a schoolboy was corresponding with British Museum Keepers of Antiquities. In 1850 he became a member of the Archaeological Institute in his first year at Balliol College Oxford. It will have been during vacation time that he met up and worked with WJJB, and subsequently he submitted a few articles which were published in *Norfolk Archaeology*.

He followed his father into holy orders and entered into 'an arduous incumbency' in a slum parish in Sheffield where he was enormously successful, increasing his congregation into the hundreds from a starting point of six. He is remembered for his kindness, and for his efforts to improve the circumstances of his impoverished parishioners, but at the age of thirty-five he resigned, having worn himself out in their service.

His mother had died and left him an income in trust that enabled him to travel. He went out to Egypt for the sake of his health, and it was from there that he started a second career, as a traveller and collector. He made extensive expeditions in Egypt, on foot, on donkeys and on camels. He settled in at the Luxor Hotel and made himself available at teatime for local dealers, and regular commercial transactions took place.

Over many years he collected vast quantities of small Egyptology which he brought back to England. The British Museum, and the Ashmolean Museum in Oxford, house many thousands of objects bought from Chester at a small profit to him or were donated by him. The Ashmolean has, in their Egyptian galleries, a Chester Room in memory of his contribution.

Slag as found at Horstead and Buxton by Mr Chester

Pits are the most unsatisfactory things archaeologists can have to do with, at least I think so. The above two or rather they look like two, promised some reward for the terrible opening as their form was regular and conical not quite so bowl-shaped as usual. The one we opened measured about 16 or 17 feet and five feet in depth. The sides of some part we examined was ... as usual with stone very compact but on the other side broken by digging ... after excavating 11 foot of mould the soil was firmer and we came to stones and amongst the stones I found several pieces of slag (the slag heap is within a few yards) and beyond burnt earth and stones and the further we dug the more charcoal and darker it became until we have ... for 8 or 9 feet when the soil altered in colour still retaining a darker shade.

Mr Chester is clearly the Rev. Greville Chester B.A. who in *Norfolk Archaeology V* communicated 'An account of the discovery of Ancient British Remains near Cromer'. Three sentences are relevant. 'The numerous pits – the presumed vestiges of ancient British villages – and the Roman kiln found near Sheringham by Mr Bolding, have already been described in papers before our society ... Three Halfpenny Hill was partially examined in 1849 by Mr Bolding and some other members of the society (WJJB was Director of Fieldwork). ... In August 1850, I opened the adjacent tumulus called Three Farthing Hill' (out of which an urn measuring 17½ ins in height, 13ins across the mouth, 3ft 10ins round the widest part and 22ins round the bottom was presented to the Norwich Museum). The 1704 map of Weybourne had clearly inspired WJJB. South of the village, on gently rising ground, the map showed a medieval moat fed by a spring, with a channel joining the Spring Beck, which ran on to supply the water for the watermill near the beach. In his archaeological notebook WJJB did a plan of the moat and alongside it some writing: 'Hall Yds as it was 150 years ago. (i.e. as shown on the 1704 map). Dotted lines the present road and fence Black marks where Roman pottery was found No.1 No. 2 Roman remains under the surface not yet excavated I think the tongue marked 3. has been raised since the moat as it is artificial and there are no Roman remains except very ... say 4 feet that is I have dug a hole to that depth and I have not found any ... The interior of the moat contains about half an acre.'

Today the moat is seen from the road up to Kelling Heath and Holt as a rectangular copse in the middle of an agricultural field.

In *Norfolk Archaeology Volume III* (1852) there is an article by 'Henry Harrod Esq., Hon. Secretary' entitled, "On the Weybourne Pits". The first paragraph, as a statement of the changing world, is worth recording:

A few years ago, the task of investigating the primaeval antiquities

The urn found in a barrow on Salthouse Common August 1850.

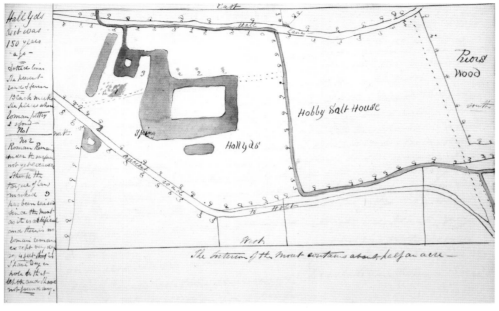

'Hall Yds as it was 150 years ago' (see page 159).

of this county, would have been very difficult one: the works on antiquarian subjects were scarce and expensive; and the opportunities of visiting authenticated vestiges in other places rarely offered themselves, except to a man of wealth and leisure. Now, however, it is different: the increased facilities afforded by railways for traversing the kingdom at a quick and cheap rate, and the records of investigations and discoveries, which the labours of the metropolitan and provincial societies, and the zeal and munificence of private individuals, have produced, have very much decreased the cost and labour of the archaeologist". As railway travel out of Norfolk had only become available in 1845 it is clear that the gentlemen archaeologists in the county were quick off the mark to avail themselves of the new opportunities. Harrod's article covered much wider ground than the pits in the immediate vicinity and it is clear that he used some of WJJB's findings in other parts of Norfolk to help expand his writing, and he even refers to findings in Yorkshire, Derbyshire and Wiltshire.

WJJB gets several mentions in the article, the first of which acknowledges his plan of the siting of the pits which was produced in lithographic form by Henry Ninham: 'The map, made from actual survey by my friend, Mr Bolding, of Weybourne, shows the position and arrangement of the pits existing on the high ground above the valley, in which the village is placed'. The tumuli on Salthouse Heath have a mention. One was opened by Mr G.Chester (*mentioned earlier in WJJB's notes*). 'It produced, about two feet from the surface, a very large and rude urn of a brown clay, containing a quantity of burnt bones. This he has kindly presented to the Norwich Museum. A much more perfect tumulus, opened by Mr Bolding and myself, produced only a very small Celtic urn, which was broken to pieces by the spade.'

Volume IV of *Norfolk Archaeology* has in the minutes of the meeting on 5th February 1852 that, 'W.J.J.Bolding of Weybourne communicated the discovery of an immense quantity of fragments of Celtic and Roman pottery in trenching the site of 'Salthouse Broad' on the NE coast between Cley and Weybourne. A deputation of the Committee, at Mr Bolding's invitation, subsequently visited the spot, which is separated from the sea by the sand-bank known as the 'Marram Hills', when a hill adjoining, called Greenborough Hill, was excavated, and also found to have numerous fragments of Roman pottery, a few Roman bricks, and considerable traces of fire.'

Only on one occasion did WJJB have an article published in *Norfolk Archaeology*, in Volume V (1859). Not surprisingly it was on a discovery found in his own parish and was dated by him as March 1857:**'Notice of an Ancient Potter's Kiln discovered in the Parish of Weybourne, in the Hundred of Holt,** 'communicated by William J.J.Bolding Esq.

A POTTERS KILN WEYBOURNE.

'A POTTERS KILN WEYBOURNE' A sketch by an unknown artist representing the Romano-British pottery kiln excavated by WJJB in March 1857,which was published in *Norfolk Archaeology* Volume V (1859) to illustrate WJJB's article.

'Between two fields, not far from the east boundary of the parish of Weybourne, in the Hundred of Holt, there is a chalk-pit which appears to have been occasionally used for agricultural purposes. The soil resting on the chalk showed no marks of difference from the rest of the field; but on walking past the face of the steep bank I fancied some of the chalk was darker, and had been disturbed. On examination I found some pieces of Roman pottery, and determined on a farther investigation. The following notes are the result.

The outline of the disturbed soil represented a bowl-shaped pit about four feet in depth and twenty feet in diameter if formed into a complete circle, and nearly flat at the bottom. Of this bowl the chalk-pit formed a section, nearly in the middle.

I commenced by digging in a slanting direction from the surface, and soon came upon what appeared to be a circle of broken pottery, cemented with brick-earth, which had evidently been subjected to the action of fire. Gradually a circular table, surrounded by a flue and a fireplace, was laid bare and which I think could have been nothing else than a Romano-British potter's kiln.

This kiln differs in many respects from those described by Mr Artis and others, and as this is the only instance of remains of the kind being found in the County, a further minute description of them may be interesting.

The ware was all of that dull blue kind which is usually found, except the fragments built into the kiln itself, and from them the colour had been driven off by the intense heat. The bottoms of the vessels must have varied very much in size – from one inch and a half to ten or twelve inches, perhaps more. There was very little attempt at ornament on any of them; and out of about fifty pieces which I collected, two or three had foliated patterns upon them, which ran round the bowl below the rim. One or two other pieces, which formed the side of the bowl, were indented by marks such as would be represented by the fingernail in soft clay; these marks were very similar to those visible on the Saxon pottery, which has been found on the neighbouring Salthouse marshes, and which of an inferior kind, bearing no marks of the lathe. There were no fragments of bricks. The kiln itself was coloured a deep blue-black, so were the pieces of wrappers or outer coverings. It had evidently been used more than once before the inside circle of fragments of brick-earth had been added, and it had been used after the addition, as both brick-earth and pottery were stained with the colouring matter. Although the heat had been strong enough to destroy the colour of the pieces of pottery used, it had not penetrated to the outer circle. The construction of the kiln appeared to me to be this: an excavation was formed, flat at the bottom, on which was marked the outer circle, five feet in diameter; from the same centre a circle, two feet in diameter, formed the table; by removing the earth from the immediate space to the depth of ten inches a flue was thus constructed; the outer circle was broken into, and gradually inclined a few inches for the fire-place; the whole was then washed with a thin coating of slip; the pottery packed in the shape of a dome, covered with wrappers, a vent being left at the top of the dome; fired and coloured. The flue when opened by me had been reduced in width six inches by the juxta-position of broken fragments, and an addition had been made to the table close to the fire-place, evidently after the kiln had been used once, by placing broken fragments of pottery and brick-earth by the side of it; for what purpose it is not easy to say, but most probably for the purpose of forming a second table on which to pile smaller ware, which could not readily be packed over so wide a space as the first and larger flue.

There is little clay and not much brick-earth in the parish of Weybourne; what there is is of an inferior description. There are, however, some fissures, or pockets in the chalk filled with a better kind of earth, and apparently one of these places had been taken advantage of in which to make the ware.'

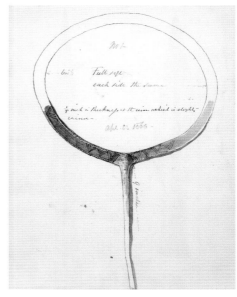

Quoit-headed pin from the later Bronze Age (800 B.C. or older) grey wash and ink drawing in WJJB's archaeological notebook dated 23 April 1866.

WJJB's sketchbook, which includes some archaeological notes, extracts of which have been quoted above, has two grey wash and ink drawings. They are both dated in pencil April 23rd 1866. The first (No. 1) is of a Bronze Age quoit-headed pin. WJJB drew it full size (6¼ ins across) 'each side the same' and '1/8 inch in thickness at the rim which is slightly raised'. The other drawing is of two Bronze Age spear heads (No. 2 and No. 3). There is no more information and therefore one is none the wiser as to where they came from.

From the evidence it seems clear that WJJB retained an interest in archaeology right up to the end of his life. The Norfolk and Norwich Archaeological Society Report for 1900 recorded, 'Died, Mr W.J.J.Bolding, who possessed a most extensive knowledge of the archaeology of the district in and around Weybourne.'

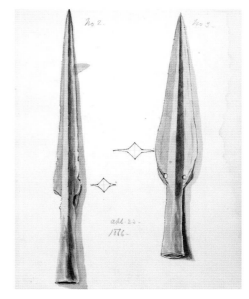

Two Bronze Age spear heads. Grey wash and ink drawing 23 April 1866.

Appendix II

1891 – Four and a half days at Blakeney

Monday January 19th. Started from Weybourne after an early breakfast and walked round to the 'Villa' by Cley. The day was just breaking and a sharp frost. A small bunch of widgeon got up not far from where our punt are kept and a good lot of duck came off the land. Got underway at high water, 9 am (a moderate breeze East) I shoved along south side. Just before I got to the shingle point a small bunch of widgeon, followed by about 40, came from the Beachway and hit my side of the Hood - got well up wind to them, sitting all over the place - shot when they rose - downed 8. Loaded and went up Beachway , water falling fast. Several fowl afloat and on the wing – had a rare time getting up a nearly dry creek, tipped and fired a very awkward shot – downed 2 duck 1 widgeon. Went over to the Freshes and shot 2 mergansers out of 3 with punt gun, also 4 knot, I god-wit with handgun. Returned to the 'Villa' well satisfied.

Bag: 2 duck, 9 widgeon, 2 mergansers, 4 knot, 1 godwit

Tuesday January 20th. Turned out at daylight, very strong wind East and sharp frost.

Several bunches of widgeon on the wing. Started for Beachway. Just off the Hood 6 duck came straight at me and lit in the slog not more than 150 yards off. Paddled to them and got 4 when they rose. Several fowl flying about Beachway. Made out 6 in the water. Shot when they rose bagging 2 duck 2 widgeon. Too much sea to cross to the Freshes. On the way back shot at 2 scaup and got 1 and stopped the other with hand gun when he came past me. Had a good dinner. The 'Villa' beginning to look very nice - went out at night – very dark- shot close to the 'Villa' by sound. Felt certain I killed some, but couldn't find any.

Bag: 6 duck 2 widgeon 2 scaup

Wednesday January 21st. Same old wind. Marshall picked up 4 widgeon round the Hood that I shot the night before. Ran down in a lot of slog* at a bunch of scaup. On north side and got 7. Got back to Weybourne as I was shooting with Walpole (Presumably Lord Walpole of Wolterton, Lord of the Manor of Weybourne) the next day.

Bag: 7 scaup 4 widgeon

Friday January 23rd. Glass very low and snowing hard. Hannay Upcher had asked me to his to dine and sleep, Didn't know what to do. At last Blakeney got the mastery but arrived there too late. There had been a swarm of fowl about. G.Long got 2 shots coming up from the lifeboat drill* and old Arthur made a good day's work. Went out at 10 pm. Tide just beginning to run the flats. Got 5 widgeon on "our manor" and again 3 Returned to the 'Villa'.

Bag: 8 widgeon

Saturday January 24th. Lovely morning slight frost light air of wind SW Went down at low water. Tried to get a couple of scaup together but couldn't. so didn't shoot. Shot at 1 with hand gun and stopped him, but he afterwards got up and flew away. Saw old Long at the Freshes and G.Long coming up the narrows. Went on board G.Long's smack and smoked a pipe below. Long went on deck and saw 4 scaup swimming up the narrows. I went at them and went all together pulled but the gun missed. Put on another cap and it missed again. Tried to prime but up they got. I couldn't understand the gun missing. Primed again and went at a single scaup in the sky. After a great deal of cracking and hissing off she went and so did the duck. When loading I found there was a big piece of oakum in the breech which had been left there when I wiped out the night before and sufficiently accounted for the misfire. Lots of duck and brent flying west. Saw old Arthur further on trying to get up to some brent and widgeon but no go. Went with him at a good lot of widgeon but they rose wild and I didn't get any. He was off them and I didn't shoot. Bishop went to the Freshes and I on to Blackrock – shot at 4 widgeon and got 3. Again at a scattered bunch of 6 – the old brent wouldn't let me look at them. Returned to the 'Villa' having had a good day's work and then home.

Bag: 9 widgeon

Four days and a piece: 32 widgeon 8 duck 9 scaup 2 mergansers 1 godwit 51 fowl average at 12 per diem. Best average in Holland had been 26 from 2 guns. Good on yer old Blakeney.

Next time down shot in narrows with George Long and Harry Long at about 2 dozen whoopers. Stopping 10 and getting 8 swans 1 cygnet.

Appendix III

W.J.J. Bolding's Will

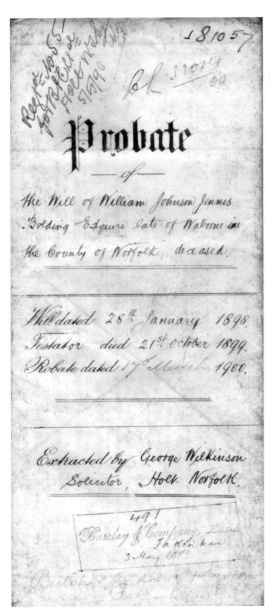

Wills are a great source of information and WJJB's, dated 28th January 1898, is no exception. As expected William Bolding Monement was to inherit the Weybourne estate, with a legacy of four thousand pounds: 'I bequeath all my furniture, plate, linen, china and other household effects not by me otherwise disposed of, my horses, carriages, harness and other effects in and about the house and grounds now in my occupation and all my live and dead stock and crops of corn and grain on and about my farm at Waborne'. Frank would inherit all his Cley properties and land: 'all the live and dead farming stock and crops and grain on and about my farm', with a legacy of two thousand pounds. For the four spinster nieces, 'the house garden land and premises in Waborne aforesaid ('The Cottage') now in the occupation of my four unmarried nieces, daughters of my deceased sister Esther Monement with the house and garden adjoining now in the occupation of John Lyles; a portion of my piece of land in Waborne aforesaid called Swallows with the barn and other buildings thereon the said portion being such part of the said piece of land as lies to the east and south of the said barn and buildings as the Cottage with the garden and appurtenances in Waborne aforesaid now in the occupation of Robert Digby; my cottages, fish house with the appurtenances and the two pieces of land and roadway in Sheringham in the said county and my cottages and land at Gresham in the said county to my unmarried nieces so long as they shall respectively continue unmarried with the remainder to the survivor of my said unmarried nieces in fee simple'. The nieces were certainly able to 'live off own means' for the rest of their lives. John Bolding (John Francis Bolding Monement) in Australia was to receive the income from a trust fund, which would then be divided between his children after his death. Hannah Beatrice Goble and Maude Marguerite Bowden-Smith would receive a legacy of six hundred pounds, as would their unmarried siblings. 'To such children of my said niece Hannah Beatrice Goble as shall be living at my decease and shall attain the age of twenty-one years the legacy or sum of three hundred pounds free from legacy duty in equal shares. To the child of my said niece Maud Marguerite Bowden-Smith the legacy or sum of one hundred pounds free from legacy duty'.

William Cooke, WJJB's loyal gardener first employed back in the 1840s to receive 'the legacy or sum of ten pounds free from legacy duty'. The only other non family person mentioned was 'To my nurse E.S.Doble the legacy or sum of twenty pounds free from legacy duty'. She had been in 'The House' in the 1891 Census and will have nursed Hannah in her last illness, before easing the failing health of WJJB himself.

Some personal family bequests were made as one would expect: 'to my niece Rose Cicely Monement my lenses, cameras and other photographic apparatus'. Well, she was the photographer niece. 'To my nieces Rose Cicely Monement and Hannah Beatrice Goble all my painting materials equally between them'. It was not surprising that 'To my nephew William Bolding Monement such one of my two gold watches as he shall select, to my nephew Francis William Monement (Frank) the other of my gold watches and my diamond ring'. (Probably his mother's engagement ring. Frank was recently married and William Bolding Monement was a bachelor).

A number of specific bequests to nieces help to show the huge range of WJJB's interests. 'To my niece Eleanor Bolding Monement my basket with the old coins and other curiosities therein'. (About fifty assorted Roman coins have come down to the family into the 21st century). 'To my niece Hannah Beatrice Goble my case with collection of butterflies and other insects therein and my polished stones'. And to show that WJJB's sketching trip to Switzerland had other interests: 'To my niece Maud Marguerite Bowden-Smith my Swiss collection of fossils'.

FAMILY TREE SHOWING THE JENNIS, BOLDING AND MONEMENT

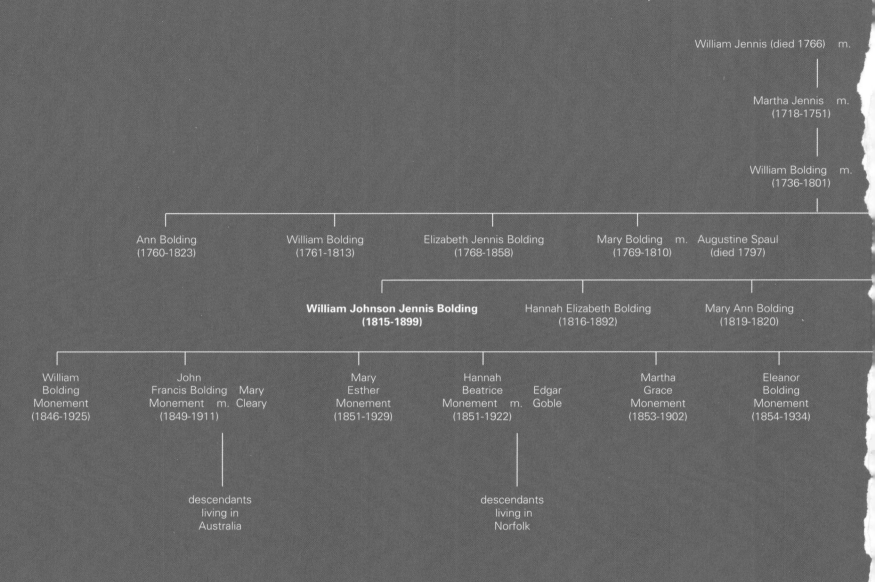

William Jennis (died 1766)   m.

Martha Jennis   m.
(1718-1751)

William Bolding   m.
(1736-1801)

Ann Bolding
(1760-1823)

William Bolding
(1761-1813)

Elizabeth Jennis Bolding
(1768-1858)

Mary Bolding   m.   Augustine Spaul
(1769-1810)   (died 1797)

William Johnson Jennis Bolding
(1815-1899)

Hannah Elizabeth Bolding
(1816-1892)

Mary Ann Bolding
(1819-1820)

William
Bolding
Monement
(1846-1925)

John
Francis Bolding   Mary
Monement   m. Cleary
(1849-1911)

Mary
Esther
Monement
(1851-1929)

Hannah
Beatrice   Edgar
Monement   m.   Goble
(1851-1922)

Martha
Grace
Monement
(1853-1902)

Eleanor
Bolding
Monement
(1854-1934)

descendants
living in
Australia

descendants
living in
Norfolk